WOLFHART PANNENBERG & RELIGIOUS PHILOSOPHY

David McKenzie

University Press of America

Copyright © 1980 by

University Press of America, Inc.

4720 Boston Way, Lanham, MD 20801

Printed in the United States of America

ISBN: 0-8191-1314-X (Case)

0-8191-1315-8 (Perfect)

Library of Congress Catalog Card Number: 80-8171

To

Janet, Sean, and Andrea

iii

ACKNOWLEDGEMENTS

I would like to acknowledge Pannenberg's permission to quote from his works, and also the permission granted by the following publishers to use previously published articles and excerpts from works on which they hold the copyright:

The Journal of Religion and the University of Chicago Press, for permission to reprint my article, "Pannenberg on God and Freedom." Copyright 1980, The University of Chicago Press.

Fortress Press, for permission to quote from What is Man?, by Wolfhart Pannenberg, 1970; and Basic Questions in Theology, Vols. 1 and 2, by Wolfhart Pannenberg, 1970-71.

Dialog and the Lutheran Theological Seminary, for permission to reprint my article, "Pannenberg on Faith and Reason."

Westminster Press, for permission to quote from The Idea of God and Human Freedom, by Wolfhart Pannenberg, Copyright 1973; Jesus--God and Man, by Wolfhart Pannenberg, Copyright 1968; Human Nature, Election, and History, by Wolfhart Pannenberg, Copyright 1977; Theology and the Kingdom of God, by Wolfhart Pannenberg, Copyright 1969; Theology and the Philosophy of Science, by Wolfhart Pannenberg, Copyright 1976; and The Theology of Wolfhart Pannenberg, by Frank Tupper, Copyright 1972.

TABLE OF CONTENTS

PREFACE xi

INTRODUCTION 1

I.   FAITH AND REASON 9

II. LANGUAGE AND HERMENEUTICS 23

     Hermeneutics, Context, and Meaning . . 23
     Hermeneutics, Context, and Truth . . . 28
     Analogy, Context, and Verifiability . 36

III. THEOLOGY AS A SCIENCE 51

     A Science of God 51
     Confirmation in Theology 55
     Difficulties in Pannenberg's Approach 64

IV. THE RESURRECTION ARGUMENT 75

     The Meaning of 'Resurrection' 77
     Historical Considerations 81
     Philosophical Considerations 84
     General Assessment of the Argument . . 99

V.   GOD AND FREEDOM 109

     Human Freedom 110
     The Theistic God and Freedom 111
     Autonomy and Freedom 116
     Divine Futurity and Human Freedom . . 118
     Problems in Pannenberg's Account . . . 123

CONCLUSION 143

BIBLIOGRAPHY 147

INDEX 155

ABBREVIATIONS USED IN NOTES

BQT . . . . . Pannenberg, Wolfhart. Basic Questions in Theology. 3 vols. Vols. 1 and 2 translated by George H. Kehm. Philadelphia: Fortress Press, 1970-71. Vol. 3 translated by R. A. Wilson. London: SCM Press, 1973. Vol. 3 also published under the title, The Idea of God and Human Freedom. Philadelphia: Westminster Press, 1973.

JGM . . . . . Pannenberg, Wolfhart. Jesus--God and Man. Translated by Lewis L. Wilkins and Duane A. Priebe. Philadelphia: Westminster Press, 1968.

TKG . . . . . Pannenberg, Wolfhart. Theology and the Kingdom of God. Edited by Richard John Neuhaus. Philadelphia: Westminster Press, 1969.

TPS . . . . . Pannenberg, Wolfhart. Theology and the Philosophy of Science. Translated by Francis McDonagh. Philadelphia: Westminster Press, 1976.

PREFACE

Much of the material contained herein represents an extensive revision of my doctoral dissertation, "The Rational Theology of Wolfhart Pannenberg," completed at the University of Texas in 1977. Two of the chapters have been published already as articles ("Pannenberg on Faith and Reason," in Dialog (Summer 1979), and "Pannenberg on God and Freedom," in The Journal of Religion (July 1980)). The other three chapters as well as the introduction and conclusion are published here for the first time.

Numerous professors, friends, and students have been of assistance to me in this project. Most obviously, all of the members of my dissertation committee left their imprint on the essay, and I would like to express my appreciation for their contributions. I am, of course, most indebted to the director of the dissertation, Professor Thomas Seung, for the criticisms and suggestions which he offered throughout. Also, Professors Aloysius Martinich, Alexander von Schoenborn, and Robert Kane from the University of Texas and Professor Merwyn Johnson of the Austin Presbyterian Theological Seminary made very helpful suggestions.

Beyond the confines of the dissertation committee, I wish to express my gratitude to Professor Eric Rust of the Southern Baptist Theological Seminary, under whose direction I formulated many of the ideas which make up my own philosophy of religion.

I would also like to acknowledge the enrichment which has come to my life as well as my work through the study of Pannenberg's thought. Though I raise what seem to me to be significant questions regarding his work, I must confess from the outset that I think the breadth of his vision and the novelty of his insights on many issues to be simply amazing.

Also, I would like to thank my colleagues, Bill Hoyt and Jorge Gonzalez, of the Berry College Department of Religion and Philosophy, for their interaction with me on numerous ideas and their support and encouragement of my work.

In addition to this academic assistance and the inspiration from Pannenberg himself, I would like to express my heartfelt gratitude to my family members for their patience and support, especially to my wife Janet, who worked very hard to provide for our family in a financial as well as a spiritual way during my years of graduate study.

INTRODUCTION

During the past two decades, few theologians have written on such a large number of issues with such intellectual rigor as Wolfhart Pannenberg. He has yet to put forward his theology in a thoroughly systematic fashion, but he has published numerous articles and several major works on topics of considerable interest to those who are familiar with the questions of religious philosophy. So far, no one has published a critical analysis of his very provocative contributions in the philosophy of religion. I believe the contributions are important enough to warrant a response. Hence the essay at hand.

The details of Pannenberg's life are by now familiar to most in the theological community though probably not so much to those in the philosophical community. Readers who are not familiar with the biographical material may refer to Frank Tupper's work, The Theology of Wolfhart Pannenberg (Philadelphia: Westminster Press, 1973), or to the biography supplied by Richard John Neuhaus in his Introduction to Pannenberg's book, Theology and the Kingdom of God (Philadelphia: Westminster Press, 1969). Pannenberg is currently Professor of Systematic Theology and Head of the Ecumenical Institute at the Protestant Faculty of Munich University.

To this point, he has produced three major works. The first of these, Jesus--God and Man (German edition: Grundzüge der Christologie, published in 1964), is mainly a theological treatise. It was the first of Pannenberg's books to appear in English (1968), and is probably the best-known of all his writings. The second, Basic Questions of Theology (a compilation of material primarily from the German works, Grundfragen systematischer Theologie, published in

1

1967, and Gottesgedanke und menschliche Freiheit, published in 1971), contains a selection of articles focused generally on certain issues in the philosophy of religion, such as the faith-reason controversy, the question of theological and religious language, and the concept of God. The third work, Theology and the Philosophy of Science (German edition: Wissenschaftstheorie und Theologie, published in 1973) is a detailed inquiry into the theoretical underpinnings of theology. Pannenberg is especially interested here in the question to what extent theology might be considered a science. In addition to these major works, he has written several other books on both theological and philosophical topics.

Pannenberg works in the context of the Protestant theological community, and considers himself responsible to the tradition of Christian thought. At the same time, however, his orientation is heavily in the direction of reason as opposed to the faith-orientation which has largely characterized contemporary Protestant theology. Indeed, the one title which best captures the mood of his work is 'theology of reason'. He believes that theology should be worked out in the marketplace of ideas and that the claims of theologians should be criticized in basically the same fashion as the claims of spokespersons from any other disciplines. Theology should have no private refuge, he thinks, where it might be immune to critical reflection.[1]

One can be rational, of course, in many different ways. Pannenberg's brand of rationality is characterized first by a strong empirical bent, a trait which has caused him to be more interested than many other continental theologians in logical positivism and analytic philosophy. Second, he exhibits something of a skeptical attitude regarding the possibilities of knowledge in all fields, including theology. Truth-claims of a theological sort, he says, can have at best only a provisional status. Traditionally, theologians have often held that

2

religious commitment requires absolute certainty. Pannenberg holds, in contrast, that modern individuals can hope for no more than a commitment based on a rational assessment of probabilities.[2] This emphasis on the provisional nature of human knowledge goes along with a third characteristic. Pannenberg espouses a kind of historical relativism in which the possibilities for truth are thought to change in accord with the passing of time and the altering of circumstances. But at the same time--and this is a fourth trait--he aspires to a comprehensive and systematic understanding of reality, very much like the traditional metaphysician. The emphases on system, context, and history show the strong Hegelian tenor in his thought. Pannenberg shares Hegel's belief that there can be an ultimate synthesis of truth which covers the whole of history, though he insists that such a synthesis is not available except in a 'proleptic' and provisional fashion within history. Thus, the future is an essential feature of Pannenberg's particular kind of historicism. Since all of our temporal systems are projections of the ultimate truth of the entire historical process, a process which is at any time incomplete, the future takes on, as he puts it, an "ontological primacy."

As with any thinker who makes significant contributions in many different areas, one of the most difficult problems for the critic is to select issues for focal study. Certain principles of selection have been operative in the present work. I have attempted first, of course, to include for analysis those issues on which Pannenberg has written most extensively. Also, I have attempted to focus on the issues which seem to me to make the most direct contact with the history of religious philosophy as well as contemporary discussions in the same area. And last, I have attempted to include the issues in regard to which Pannenberg has done his most provocative work to this point. Using these principles, I have selected for concentration five areas: (1) faith and reason, (2) language and hermeneutics, (3) theology as a science, (4) the Resurrection argument, and (5) the relation between divine power and human freedom.

I find Pannenberg's work on the issue of faith and reason to be especially helpful, and thus begin with a brief treatment of it. Due to the influence of Barth and Bultmann in the theological community and Kant in the philosophical community, there has been in the twentieth century a decided distrust of reason in Protestant theology, and a virtual disdain for the natural theology of Catholic tradition. Pannenberg attempts to appropriate for modern Protestant theology many of the arguments put forward in the tradition of natural theology, though always in a revised fashion, while striving to secure at the same time the fundamental role which has always been reserved for revelation in Protestant thought. For this if for nothing else, his work is of vital importance for contemporary philosophy of religion.

On language and hermeneutics, Pannenberg develops his contextual theory of meaning and truth for theological statements. I argue that his theory makes contact very well with contemporary currents in both analytic philosophy and modern hermeneutical discussions, but that there is a tension between the way in which Pannenberg treats the traditional doctrine of analogy and the approach which he takes to the issue of the verifiability of theological statements. With slight adjustment to accomodate the doctrine of analogy, I think that his contextual theory has abiding significance as a theological appropriation of contemporary developments in philosophy.

On the idea of theology as a science, Pannenberg attempts to show that the logical status of theological claims is not so different from that of claims made in the natural and social sciences, and that it is possible, therefore, to think of theology as a science with competing truth-claims whose truth or falsity may be decided by reference to established and accepted criteria. I argue in this regard that the testing procedure for theological statements which is suggested by Pannenberg may be able to show the determinative power of the Christian faith for the modern world but that it cannot really show the truth of that or any other tradition. I suggest that it is better not to think of theology as a science, at least as the term 'science' is normally understood, because like philosophy it does not have the requisite testing procedures for conflicting claims.

In my opinion, some of Pannenberg's most insightful and helpful work can be found in his treatment of the Resurrection. He attempts here to show that belief in the Resurrection is not incompatible with the basic commitments of modern science, historiography, and philosophy, and that these commitments in fact require such belief if their implications are pursued rigorously. I follow Pannenberg in holding that the supposed incompatibility actually does not exist, that belief in the Resurrection does not amount in effect to a sacrifice of the intellect, but I stop short of the stronger claim that the commitments of modern intellectual life actually require acceptance of the Resurrection.

Finally, Pannenberg's work on the concept of God is both extremely provocative and very problematic. I think that if there is a basic kind of tension in his thought, it is most readily apparent here. Pannenberg struggles heroically to accomodate human freedom in a universe with the sovereign God of biblical religion. I suggest that his argument leads in the direction of process philosophy, and that Pannenberg is unwilling to countenance the latter because he

5

suspects that it sacrifices the sovereignty of God for human freedom. I think that in the final analysis his synthesis here does not work, and that he is forced to fall back on the omnipotence of God at the expense of human freedom.

In regard to each of these issues, I regard Pannenberg's work as the most stimulating of all the work being done by contemporary theologians insofar as their work relates to the philosophy of religion, basically because of the expanse of his vision. He works as a theologian with unusual competence in the issues of religious philosophy, and he approaches these questions in the informed fashion of a historical theologian. I find his work in part successful, in part not, but always fascinating. Now to the issues themselves.

NOTES

[1]TKG, p. 15 (from the Introduction by Neuhaus).

[2]Ibid., p. 20.

Chapter One

FAITH AND REASON

Although Pannenberg's general intention to regain contact with the philosophical tradition of rationality is clear, it is not altogether clear how his theology of reason respects the perennial Protestant focus on faith. In this chapter, I work out the relation between faith and reason which seems to me to be implicit, though never spelled out in so many words, in Pannenberg's writings to this point.

To begin with, we should note that he criticizes the dialectical theology of Barth and Bultmann essentially for failing to give enough attention to a rational justification for belief. He is particularly outspoken in his attack on Barth. The theology of the Word of God is, he says, an extreme form of "subjectivism in theology," an example of "irrational subjectivity."[1] Barth withdrew, according to Pannenberg, from the real problems of the twentieth century into a world of "biblical supernaturalism." He attempted to do theology "from above," or from the side of God, and fell into the "hopeless" and "self-inflicted isolation of a higher glossolalia."[2] Pannenberg is more generous in his assessment of Bultmann, but says that with his existential theology he "retreated" from the crucial questions of contemporary theology, the most basic of which is how to speak of God at all.[3] Further, Hans Alberg's accusation that modern theology (and he is reflecting specifically here on Bultmann's idea of the 'nonobjectifiability' of God) has altered its conception of God in such a way as to make it safe from all criticism, and has embarked thus on an "immunization-strategy" (Immunisierungsstrategie), is "largely unanswerable."[4] Even more caustically, Pannenberg says that the neglect of philosophical theology in the work of Barth and Bultmann has had disastrous consequences for theology, that in fact the 'death of god' theologians are the "heirs" of dialectical theology.[5]

It is well-known that Barth and Bultmann were attempting to unfold the epistemological implications of the Protestant principle of justification by faith alone. As they interpreted the principle, it precludes altogether a 'natural theology' in which a rational foundation for faith is provided. Faith needs no support except the revelation of God, according to both Barth and Bultmann, and any attempt to provide support in the form of arguments is nothing other than human self-assertion in a domain which rightfully contains only the activity of God.

Pannenberg, in contrast, does not accept the denigration of natural theology which was characteristic of the dialectical theologians. He welcomes debate regarding the truth of the Christian faith and proffers a variety of rather ingenious arguments in that regard himself. At the same time, however, he attempts to preserve the privileged status accorded to revelation and faith in the Protestant tradition.

To understand Pannenberg's position, it is important first, of course, to grasp the concepts of reason and faith which he wishes to correlate. He discusses the concept of reason primarily in his article, "Faith and Reason," and the notion of faith in the article, "Insight and Faith."[6] In the former article, three views of reason are distinguished. In the first place, he says, there is an approach which might be labeled "apriori reason." Pannenberg associates this way of being rational with the thought of Aristotle, Thomas Aquinas, and Kant. In such a conception, thought begins with general principles which are immediately evident, and knowledge becomes possible through the application of these principles to the data of experience. It was this understanding of reason, says Pannenberg, to which Luther opposed faith.[7] Such a move was necessary,

he suggests, for the "contents of the Christian
faith could not be derived from these apriori
principles."[8] Statements of faith had to be
regarded as supernatural truths delivered through
revelation. Pannenberg maintains that this
arrangement of natural reason and supernaturally-
illuminated reason has always been ineffective.

The truths of faith imposed as supernatural
principles are always felt, by a reason that
understands itself as knowing by means of
principles, to be nothing but fetters which
have to be struck off.[9]

In the second place, some philosophers have
opposed to apriori reason what may be referred
to as "receiving reason." This position, which
Pannenberg associates with Plato among others,
stresses the passive reception of being. At
first glance, receptive reason appears to be
fully congruent with the aims of theology, for it
could receive the revelation of God without sub-
jecting the latter to criticism. Unfortunately,
however, what this kind of reason has always
received, in Pannenberg's view, is that which is,
the eternal amid changing appearances. But religious experience, especially that which is ingredient in the Judeo-Christian heritage is, he
believes, fundamentally eschatological, or
futural. Both Jews and Christians have always
looker forward to a vindication of their hopes.
To be sure, the past and present are also important to such an understanding. Without the
Exodus, there would be little reason for the
Jewish community to look forward to the Messiah.
And without the Resurrection, there would be
little reason for the Christian community to
anticipate the Parousia. But the basic preoccupation in both faiths is futural. What is
true, in this view, is that which will be proven
true, or reliable, in the future.[10] And since
truth is futural, "it cannot be comprehended by
the sort of reason that is directed toward what

11

is contemporaneously present."[11]

In the third place, and this is the meaning which Pannenberg prefers, Hegel and Dilthey set forward the idea of "historical reason." Actually, Kant provided the point of departure for such a conception with his notion of the "productive imagination," i.e., the mental ability to synthesize a manifold of given data. Pannenberg suggests that this creative act of bringing forth something new, an effect basically of the imagination, is the fundamental character of reason.[12]

Hegel's dialectical method is especially important to Pannenberg's understanding of reason. In Hegel's procedure, historical reason consists of a progression of thought with ever new syntheses.[13] Hegel, of course, finally stops the progression with his 'absolute notion'. Pannenberg insists over against Hegel that the absolute notion contradicts the method itself because it leaves no room for further syntheses of thought.[14] Indeed, according to Pannenberg, the very fact that Hegel's system was not the final word in philosophy but has itself been taken up into further syntheses on the part of more recent thinkers points up the historical dynamic in human reason.[15]

Dilthey gave special attention to the idea of human anticipation and projection of meaning, replacing Hegel's absolute notion with the idea of the "openness of the historical mind."[16] Dilthey establishes, in effect, the unfinished nature of historical reason. Pannenberg insists that traditional metaphysics has erroneously identified the totality of meaning with the "totality of that which is."[17] But meaning always transcends that which is by including also the anticipations of what will be. The basis for these anticipations is the adumbration, or prolepsis, of meaning that may be found in the present.

12

As Pannenberg understands it, then, 'reason' should be thought of as the creative and synthetic act of the human intellect, a historical reason which is at any time still incomplete. Now let us turn to the accompanying conception of faith.

In the article mentioned above, he points out that in classical Protestant theology faith was thought to include the three elements knowledge, assent, and trust. Pannenberg has no objection to the idea that all of these elements might be included, or even that God is ultimately the source of faith in all of these senses. He is concerned, however, about the question how the elements of knowledge and trust are related. A popular opinion in contemporary theology, he says, is that the knowledge aspect of faith cannot be separated from trust as a presupposition for the latter, but is somehow grounded in the very act of trust itself.[18] That is, by making a commitment to God, one in effect opens the door for a kind of knowledge which would otherwise be unavailable.

Pannenberg allows that such a position contains a kernel of truth. But he thinks also that an important distinction is often overlooked in this connection, namely, the difference between the psychology and the logic of faith. So far as psychology is concerned, it may well be true that one's act of trust in God precedes much of his or her knowledge of God, and that through one's trust he or she becomes open to further revelation. But the relation is reversed when we speak of the <u>logic</u> of faith. Here knowledge must precede trust.[19] It would be best, Pannenberg believes, to limit the word 'faith' to the element of trust so far as logic is concerned. Faith as trust, in his conception, must be grounded in the trustworthiness of that which is trusted. And in order to assess trustworthiness, something must be known about the possible object of trust. In his view, then, faith

13

must be grounded in knowledge.

The question which must be answered now is just what kind of knowledge Pannenberg is talking about. Here he makes the move, I believe, which allows him both to remain within the general Protestant tradition and to preserve his heavily rational orientation. Pannenberg says on the one hand that the knowledge which is presupposed by faith is not different from natural knowledge. That is, it is not instilled as a special gift over and above ordinary insight. It is not a supernatural knowledge, possessed only by the elect. He makes his position in this regard quite clear: "I admit that I cannot understand any knowledge as other than 'natural'."[20] But on the other hand, he preserves a sense of continuity with the tradition by holding that only the revelation of God can be the ground for faith in the final analysis. "Only in this way is faith's vital interest in being rooted beyond itself, beyond its decision, secured."[21]

But how is it possible for faith to be based only on the revelation of God if there is no supernatural knowledge? I believe that the answer to this question can serve as a key to understanding Pannenberg's approach in general. I submit that Pannenberg wants to link natural knowledge and revelation. In other words, it is possible for faith to be based only on the revelation of God (in the absence of supernatural knowledge) just in case revelation is a self-unveiling of God which can be appropriated by any ordinary, objective observer through his or her historical knowledge. So conceived, it is true that revelation is the basis for faith; and, since revelation can be appropriated by human knowledge, it is also true that faith presupposes knowledge.

It is interesting to note that Pannenberg makes contact here with the old Lutheran

rationalism of the seventeenth century, the
scholastic period in Protestant thought. Many
of the theologians of that time accepted natural
theology alongside the 'revealed theology' contained in Scripture. And they attempted in a
variety of ways to provide a rational justification for the truths of faith which would not
depend strictly on revelation, the general
assumption being that natural knowledge is
finally harmonious with divine truth.[22] Pannenberg's approach is thus not altogether out of
keeping with the Lutheran tradition, though he
certainly goes further than the seventeenth-
century rational theologians in rejecting the
distinction between natural and revealed theology itself.

Pannenberg attempts to show his relation
to the tradition by arguing that the Protestant
Reformation was actually the means through which
a rational approach to theology became possible.
He says that the Reformation originally effected
only an alteration of authority over human
thought in that the authority of the Pope was
exchanged for the authority of the Bible. However, the general effect of the Protestant rejection of papal authority was to place the believer
in a more immediate relation to God. He is reflecting at this point on the fact that Protestants have consistently insisted that each individual should interpret Scripture for himself or
herself under the guidance of the Holy Spirit.
The believer in this way lives, in reality, only
under the authority of God alone; there is no
human or institutional authority over his or her
thought.[23]

Pannenberg suggests that the Reformation
thus implicitly contains the recognition of the
autonomy of human reason.[24] As a consequence of
the Reformation, it becomes possible for the
believer to decide by the exercise of his or her
reason what is to count as truth. Indeed, it
was only a matter of time before this idea

15

gained a stronger foothold in the form of a willingness to adopt a critical attitude even toward Scripture and the existence of God.[25] With such an extension, the initial distinction between believer and unbeliever collapses. Now every human being stands directly before the purported revelation, attempting to answer the question whether it is true.[26]

As discussions in later chapters will make clear, Pannenberg does not endorse as a positive consequence of the Reformation an absolute and unbounded freedom wherein no authority is recognized. This kind of freedom, he will argue, must receive content, or direction, to be of value, and without such is a negative consequence of the Reformation. The positive consequence which is of such significance for the present discussion is the releasement of the theological mind from finite institutional authority for the transcendent authority of divine revelation.

The upshot of these reflections, then, is that the Reformation makes possible what might be called an 'autonomous theologian' (my phrase, not Pannenberg's) and thereby the development of a rational theology.[27] The autonomous theologian accepts only what can be justified as a reasonable projection of truth in regard to a divine revelation. He or she works without any preconceived bindings to the effect that God speaks only in Scripture or only according to Holy Tradition, and is even open to the possibility that God does not speak at all. Such an individual adopts what is tantamount to a receptive, open-minded attitude in regard to the question of the meaning of human existence. And further, the theologian must himself or herself take responsibility for the creative syntheses of the various threads of evidence available through historical and scientific inquiry. To be an autonous theologian, in other words, is simply to adopt the stance of a rational human being with respect to the question of God.

It seems to me that Pannenberg's approach to the relation of faith and reason is quite helpful in most respects. There are problems, of course, especially with the Hegelian-style identification of human knowledge and divine revelation. The main difficulty is this: So long as we use 'knowledge' in the strict sense, that is, to include only truth-claims which are indeed true, the identification in question is logically satisfactory. But in this case, we would have to ask whether there really is any specifically theological knowledge, since theological truth-claims are so widely contested. But if we use 'knowledge' in its loose, more customary fashion, that is, to include truth-claims which are widely believed to be true whether they turn out to be so in fact or not, we have to raise the question whether God would not be providing mutually inconsistent revelations on Pannenberg's assumptions; for many truth-claims which are fervently held as true by large groups of individuals conflict with others believed just as strongly, especially in religion. Probably Pannenberg would answer this objection by distinguishing the ultimate and absolute truth about God and history and the tentative truth-claims which we make at any point in time, allowing perhaps that the latter can appropriately be called 'knowledge' though there are inconsistencies due to our limited conceptual frameworks. In the light, however, of the extensive character of the inconsistencies which prevail among the multivaried theological claims of this or any other epoch, one wonders whether the term 'knowledge', which normally depicts collections of truth-claims with greater consistency, has not lost an important part of its meaning in such usage.

This question will be explored in more detail in chapter three. At this point, my primary concern is simply to present Pannenberg's basic program. Despite the difficulties, his

approach seems to be very liberating in many
respects. It allows one a kind of theological
honesty which is apt to be unavailable on other
assumptions. With this approach, one simply
cannot immunize theology. We have to pay the
price if the further development of human understanding proves our current theological positions
to be wrong. Pannenberg has provided a way in
which the theologian can both maintain open and
honest dialogue with nonbelievers as well as
members of rival religions and hold onto the
concept of the divine initiative for faith which
is so important to Protestants. And further,
of course, it enables Pannenberg to be both
a theologian and a religious philosopher, for
he is able to participate in the discussions of
philosophical issues in a philosophical fashion,
that is, with an honest, open, and free pursuit
of the truth.

[1]TPS, p. 273.

[2]"Types of Atheism and their Theological Significance," in BQT, 2:189, 199.

[3]Ibid., p. 199.

[4]Albert's charge is from his book, Traktat über kritische Vernunft, cited in TPS, p. 47, and discussed on pp. 47-50. My translation, "immunization-strategy," is based on the German text, p. 49.

[5]"Speaking about God in the face of Atheist Criticism," in BQT, 3:102.

[6]Both of these articles are in BQT, vol. 2.

[7]"Faith and Reason," in BQT, 2:56. Pannenberg does not supply a reference to Luther's work in connection with this particular point. Probably the latter's harsh comments on "human reason" in The Bondage of the Will lie behind the remark. See Martin Luther, The Bondage of the Will, trans. Philip S. Watson and Benjamin Drewery, in Luther's Works, ed. Helmut T. Lehmann, vol. 33: Career of the Reformer, III (Philadelphia: Fortress Press, 1972), pp. 120-27, 171-75, 206-11.

[8]"Faith and Reason," p. 56.   [9]Ibid., p. 57.

[10]Pannenberg is relying heavily at this point on the Hebrew idea that Jahweh proves himself to be God through the events of history, and that this proof will culminate in the great events of the future. See especially Rolf Rendtorff's essay, "The Concept of Revelation in Ancient Israel," in Revelation as History, ed. Wolfhart Pannenberg et al., trans. David Granskou (New York: Macmillan Company, 1968), pp. 30-48.

[11]"Faith and Reason," p. 59.

[12]Ibid., pp. 60-61. Actually, Pannenberg seems to combine here Kant's "reproductive imagination," which synthesizes a manifold of empirical data, and the "productive imagination," whose function is to provide an original synthesis "directed exclusively to the apriori combination of the manifold," i.e., Kant's "transcendental unity of apperception" and the "pure concepts of the understanding." See Immanuel Kant, Critique of Pure Reason, trans. Norman Kemp Smith (New York: St. Martin's Press, 1965), pp. 142-43.

[13]"Faith and Reason," pp. 60-61. The Phenomenology is, of course, supposed to be an account of the actual course of reason in history. Hegel provides a description of the method employed in the work and referred to here by Pannenberg in his Preface to the Phenomenology, pp. 85-107 in the Baillie translation (New York: Harper and Row, 1967).

[14]"Faith and Reason," pp. 60-61.

[15]Ibid.   [16]Ibid.

[17]Pannenberg discusses this basic problem in metaphysics in the essay, "Christian Theology and Philosophical Criticism," in BQT, 3:116-43, especially pp. 130-33.

[18]"Insight and Faith," in BQT, 2:28-32. These comments are directed primarily to the work of Paul Althaus.

[19]Ibid., pp. 32-33.   [20]Ibid., p. 33.

[21]Ibid., p. 38.

[22]See Heinrich Schmid's work, The Doctrinal Theology of the Evangelical Lutheran Church, trans. Charles A. Hay and Henry E. Jacobs, 3rd. ed.

(Minneapolis: Augsburg Publishing House, 1875), pp. 25-38, 103-11.

[23]_Reformation zwischen gestern und morgen_ (Gütersloher Verlagshaus Gerd Mohn, 1969), pp. 10-22.

[24]Ibid., p. 15.   [25]Ibid., pp. 16-18.

[26]In his article, "The Significance of Christianity in the Philosophy of Hegel," in BQT, 3:151-52, Pannenberg applauds Hegel for his recognition that the move from the faith of the Reformation to the rational autonomy of the Enlightenment was an "intrinsically necessary step" in the human development.

[27]Again, 'autonomous' here is used to refer only to a self-government which is independent of human and institutional authority. Ultimately, of course, Pannenberg allows that the very process of independent, creative thought is itself a kind of submission to the guidance of God.

Chapter Two

LANGUAGE AND HERMENEUTICS

Like many other theologians of recent vintage, Pannenberg attempts to defend theology against the charge that its statements are cognitively meaningless. Due to his work in the area of historical theology and his acquaintance with contemporary philosophical issues related to analytic philosophy on the one side and to phenomenology and existentialism on the other side, Pannenberg comes to the debate much better equipped than most participants. He has, for instance, not only a good understanding of the modern issue of verification in theology, but also more than a nodding acquaintance with the medieval struggle over the concept of analogy. By combining these and other strands of thought, he is able to produce a novel and creative synthesis on the issue of theological language, though there are certain problems as I shall attempt to show.

Pannenberg's work in the area is focused primarily on the development of a contextual theory of meaning and truth for theological statements. I shall set forward his position first in relation to the question of meaning and then in relation to the question of truth. After stating the core components of his position in this way, I shall relate Pannenberg's work on the contextual theory to his views on the doctrine of analogy and explore a point of tension which seems, at any rate, to be present in the relation between the two areas.

Hermeneutics, Context, and Meaning

Pannenberg notes that in modern philosophy there are basically three accounts of meaning:

23

the referential, intentional, and contextual
views. He gives short shrift to the first two,
arguing essentially that neither reference nor
intention can be settled without recourse to the
social and historical context of a statement.[1]
That reference is context-dependent does not, of
course, vitiate the entire referential account;
and again, that language is a public, cultural
and thus contextually-related phenomenon does
not vitiate the entire intentional account.
Pannenberg seeks simply to relate these two views
to the broader and more inclusive contextual
account, one which can take up the elements of
truth in the other accounts while also going
beyond them.

In his view, it was the Wittgenstein of the
Philosophical Investigations who paved the way
for a contextual account. In this work, according to Pannenberg, Wittgenstein called attention
to the importance of social context for meaning
with his well-known concept of language games.[2]
This concept implies that language has an enormous variety of functions, and that to understand
a statement means not to focus on the isolated
meanings of the individual words or phrases involved but to focus instead on the situations in
which the statement is meaningfully employed.
Though Wittgenstein's contribution is important,
in Pannenberg's opinion even the idea of language games does not usher in a thoroughgoing
contextual account of meaning. Language games
are basically "forms of life" in the Wittgen-
steinian jargon, or as Pannenberg puts it, "constant social structures." As such, he contends,
they are also abstractions. By overemphasizing
the analogy between language usage and games, he
suggests, Wittgenstein tended to lose sight of
individual variations in expression as well as
the historical developments within languages.
According to Pannenberg, an adequate account
should take into consideration not only the
relatively stable social contexts of language

games, but also the broader, historical process
in which such stable contexts arise.[3]

Pannenberg does not work through the pain-
staking semantic analyses which have characterized modern language philosophy. Instead, he
develops his theory of meaning more or less as
an offshoot of his work on theological hermeneutics. Hence, in order to get hold of the
basic ingredients of his contextualism, one must
concentrate on his discussion of hermeneutics.
Of consummate importance in this regard are two
works, one his article, "Hermeneutic and Universal History," in Basic Questions in Theology, and
the other his study of the relation between
scientific method and theology in Theology and
the Philosophy of Science.

Since Bultmann's existential hermeneutics
has been the dominant focus of recent work on
the topic, Pannenberg is primarily concerned in
this connection to set his own position over
against that of Bultmann. As is widely acknow-
ledged among commentators, Bultmann's program is
ambiguous at a crucial point: It is difficult
to decide whether his demythologized Christianity
is just a possibility for human existence or
whether it is also supposed to be a divine
address to humanity. No doubt it is supposed
to be the latter. Unfortunately, however, within
the Bultmannian framework there seems to be no
way to speak significantly of God.[4]

This difficulty in Bultmann's program does
not escape the attention of Pannenberg. In fact,
he distinguishes his own hermeneutics from that
of Bultmann precisely at this point. According
to Pannenberg, Bultmann's existential interpretation restricts the contemporary significance of
the past to "that which a transmitted text expresses concerning the question of human existence."[5] Everything in the text becomes relevant
only as a particular possibility for humanity.
Pannenberg conceeds that the biblical texts in

25

general are expressions of human possibilities; but, he argues, they also, "indeed primarily," deal with the works of God in the events of history.[6] And what they say about humanity is always "conditioned" by this prior concern with God. Thus, Bultmann's hermeneutics constricts the possibilities of the biblical texts in that it does not allow them "to say what they themselves have to say."[7]

Pannenberg's objection to Bultmann's program sounds simple enough. It appears that he just wants to "get back to God," so to speak. But the real objection is far subtler than this, and it turns directly on the idea of historical contexts of meaning. The heart of Pannenberg's objection is shown in the following statement:

> The existentialist constriction of the hermeneutic theme raises the further question of whether the historical distance (Abstand) between the texts to be understood and the interpreter's own time is retained in all its profundity if one subjects the texts to an anthropocentric understanding of existence.[8]

Bultmann's approach, Pannenberg is claiming here, does not fully appreciate the profound difference in the conceptual frameworks of the New Testament and the modern world. To be sure, Bultmann was aware of the distance, and he intended to take it into account through his program of demythologization. But in translating the New Testament preoccupation with God into a human possibility, he overlooks the difference in historical contexts of meaning. Pannenberg insists that if we seek to appreciate the New Testament focus on the divine, then we cannot simply eliminate that focus in translating. We should not, in other words, superimpose our own anthropocentric worldview on the biblical theocentricism when trying to understand what the Bible says.

26

At this point, Pannenberg picks up the original motivation for Barthian theology. His suggestion, however, is not that we should preserve the New Testament focus on God as it was originally expressed (the Barthian tendency). Rather, his point is that we should recognize the strangeness of the first-century context, and allow it to stand as it is. The interpreter, he says, should appreciate the "then-ness" (Damaligkeit) of his or her text. One should expose himself or herself to the events that occurred at that time as they were understood at that time, and only then ask what they might mean for our context. The interpreter "must apprehend the past situation to which the text refers in its disparity from his own present, and may relate this situation to the present only in its disparateness."[9]

A good example of this variation in conceptual worlds, and the difficulties which are created thereby for the interpreter, is the difference between the cosmic expectations of modern humanity and those of the first-century Hebrews. Even modern Christians are taken back by the very strong eschatological expectations of their first-century counterparts. We can understand that they had such expectations. And especially well-trained historical theologians can understand to some extent the content of the expectations through literary and historical investigations. But it is extremely difficult for us to find a point of contact with those expectations in the modern world. And it is doubtful whether any of us, even contemporary Christians, can really accept the eschatology of the New Testament as New Testament Christians accepted it. Their intense eschatological expectations remain, in a way, forever strange to us.

Bultmann, of course, translates the first-century expectations into a particular mode of present existence, namely, a life of openness to the future.[10] But this is not enough for

27

Pannenberg. He insists that an irreducible component in the relevant texts is the expectation of a divine action. And he asks then whether there is any way in which this element, strange as it is, can be incorporated into our contemporary framework. Pannenberg is thus attempting to steer a middle course between the hermeneutical views of Barth and Bultmann, a course in which the basic contributions of both can be preserved, and the gap between their work overcome.

This discussion brings into clear focus several of the chief ingredients in Pannenberg's contextual view of meaning. First, he speaks of broad and yet concrete historical contexts and not just of differing typical contexts (as in Wittgenstein's language games). Second, he insists that texts from an alien culture should be understood in terms of their original intention within that context. They may have a meaning which is bound to their native context in the sense that it depends on presuppositions which are no longer understandable or acceptable. We should not think of the text as just another instance of the sort of thing with which we are familiar (as in Bultmann's existential interpretation). And third, Pannenberg seems to envisage the possibility that an alien meaning can finally be incorporated in some way into our contemporary framework. But this cannot be done by taking over the content of the text uncritically, and refusing to allow for modifications in its basic ideas (as in Barth's theology of the Word of God).

Hermeneutics, Context, and Truth

In Pannenberg's view, not only meaning but also truth is dependent on context. It has become clear, he says, that "the truth has another form for different peoples and ages."[11] In the light of this fact, we would act "narrow-mindedly" if we identified any particular historical perspective with the absolute truth.[12] And again, "Every absolutization of a contemporary truth would at once misunderstand the historical multiplicity of pictures of the truth."[13] The upshot of this reflection is, according to Pannenberg, that "the unity of truth can now only be thought of as the history of truth," or in other words, "truth has a history and its essence is the process of this history."[14]

It should not be concluded from these comments that Pannenberg thinks of context as the sole determinant for truth. Just as his contextual account of meaning attempts to preserve the contributions of both a referential and an intentional account, so his contextual view of truth seeks to preserve the contributions of both a correspondence and a consensus theory. He makes ample use, for instance, of the widespread contemporary appreciation of the role that consensus plays in determining the truth even of empirical claims.[15] And consensus, of course, is itself a function of the general context of a claim. At the same time, however, Pannenberg backs away from an unqualified acceptance of the consensus account. "A pure consensus theory of truth. . .is incapable of accounting for the distinction between a consensus in truth and a prevailing convention."[16] Unless, in other words, assertions can be checked by reference to the relevant states of affairs, then anything could count as truth if by some means a consensus could be procured in its favor. In regard to truth, then, Pannenberg again promotes a general contextual theory which is inclusive of the most important aspects of the other prominent theories.

From our analysis so far, it sounds as though Pannenberg is attempting to be something of an epistemological relativist. Both meaning and truth, he says, depend at least to some extent on historical context. At the same time, however, it is obvious that he does not want to leave the truth of the New Testament to first-century Christians. In some way, the truth for them must also be the truth for us. Further investigation of his hermeneutics will show that the initial impression of relativism is, finally speaking, mistaken. In a move which is designed to correlate the theological tradition and the modern preoccupation with the contextually-bound character of meaning and truth, he puts forward the novel notion of an ultimate context of meaning and along with it an ultimate truth.

In this connection, Pannenberg makes use of Hans-Georg Gadamer's idea of a "fusion of horizons" (<u>Horizontverschmelzung</u>).[17] Gadamer defines 'horizon' as "the range of vision that includes everything that can be seen from a particular vantage point."[18] The vantage point here is one's intellectual perspective, the various fundamental presuppositions which one picks up from his or her general cultural situation. And the range of vision includes everything which can be understood in terms of these basic ideas. By using the concept of horizon, Gadamer is saying that an interpreter often carries along a vantage point that is radically different from that in terms of which the text was written. The concept of horizon, I believe, can be mapped nicely onto Pannenberg's idea of different historical contexts.

Gadamer stresses the notion that the different horizons of the text and the interpreter are both limited. The horizon of a text from some earlier period in the development of a tradition does not contain an understanding of everything which has transpired since the time in which it was written, and the interpreter's horizon is delimited by its own emphases and interests. The interpreter cannot simply leap over centuries of history and take up the perspective of the text. It is impossible to leave one's own presuppositions at home in this way.

How, then, is the understanding of a text from another period even possible?

According to Gadamer, understanding is possible through the interpreter's projection of a very broad, historical horizon which can be distinguished both from his own horizon and that of the text, and which allows for a fusion of these latter two.[19] The fusion does not consist in subordinating oneself to the text or in distorting the meaning of the text in order to make it conform to the modern situation. Rather, the tension between the worlds of the text and the interpreter must be brought to the fore. A fusion becomes possible only in that the horizons involved are not absolutely fixed but can be expanded in such a way as to make contact with each other. As the interpreter becomes acquainted with the distant horizon and the history of the tradition linking his own world with that of the text, there is, as Gadamer puts it, an "attainment of a higher universality" in which the particularity of both the interpreter and the text is overcome.[20]

The model which Gadamer uses throughout his discussion for this "elevation" and the consequent fusion is that of a conversation, or dialogue, between two individuals with different views. In a genuine dialogue, neither party has to subordinate his or her views to the other, and it is often possible to find some general ground for agreement. Using the conversational model, it is easy to distinguish understanding in Gadamer's sense from the kind of understanding ordinarily involved in historical studies. There is a widely-practiced study of the past in which one learns the language and general traits of a culture, and thus comes to 'understand' what various texts meant in their native setting. Historians do this sort of 'fusion' of horizons constantly. 'Fusion' here means only that one knows how to translate from one context to another. But in this sort of study, the question

31

of the truth of the text is set aside. The text
is simply "forced to abandon its claim that it
is uttering something true."[21]

In accord with the conversational model,
then, the interpreter approaches the text with
a view to its truth, and not just to understand
what it meant in its native setting. But at the
same time, the interpreter does not subordinate
his or her own horizon to that of the text. The
object is to come to an agreement, i.e., an
understanding in which one is able to move
beyond the horizonal limitations of both the
text and the interpreter's present.

Pannenberg appropriates the concept of a
Horizontverschmelzung for his own hermeneutics,
giving special stress to the finitude of the various contexts as does Gadamer. In accord with
the conversational model, he emphasizes the
necessity for an interpreter to assume a critical
stance toward the present situation, the horizon
of modern humanity. In this way, the text can
stand over against the present as an illumination
(Erhellung) of it. At the same time, however,
it is particularly important in theological hermeneutics for the interpreter to assume a critical stance also toward the horizon of the text.
Carried out in accord with this pattern, hermeneutics is a process of "productive appropriation"
of the tradition and its texts, not a mere repetition of the latter.[22]

In contrast to Gadamer, who spoke only of
a broad horizon which links the past of the text
to the present of the interpreter, Pannenberg
argues that the fusion of horizons ultimately
implies a universal horizon of meaning which includes also the future.

The text can only be understood in connection
with the totality of history which links the
past to the present, and indeed not only to
what currently exists today, but also to the

32

horizon of the future based on what is presently possible, because the meaning of the
present becomes clear only in the light of
the future.[23]

The fusion, in other words, entails a horizon
which is comprehensive enough to include the
present and past contexts as elements within it.
Pannenberg argues that such a horizon must include the future; otherwise, the limitations of
the present horizon will not be appreciated. The
only way in which Gadamer's fusion is possible,
therefore, is through the presupposition of the
ultimate, most comprehensive horizon--universal
history itself--which embraces present and past
as moments in a process which transcends both.[24]

The term 'universal history' must be clarified before further progress can be made. It
has a variety of meanings, at least two of which
seem to be behind Pannenberg's usage. It can,
for instance, mean world history, the sort of
history which one studies as a college freshman.
Or, it can mean a thoelogical overview of history
in which the sovereignty of God and the divine
plan for the salvation of humanity are empha-
sized. Or again, it can mean a philosophy of
history from a historian's standpoint in which
patterns of historical development are abstracted
from the events of world history. And then
again, it can mean a speculative philosophy of
history, such as that of Hegel and Marx, in
which the attempt is made to trace one basic,
philosophical theme through the course of historical ideologies.

Pannenberg's concept is a combination of
the theological overview and the Hegelian speculative philosophy of history. Like Hegel, he
sees the truth emerging through the process of
historical development. As we have noted, however, he does not hold, as opposed to Hegel, that
we presently have the final truth. For this reason, the present situation cannot be absolutized.

33

Pannenberg's approach is open in the sense that it appreciates the finitude of our knowledge in any given historical context. In accord with the theological overview brand of universal history, then, in his conception even the present situation is subject to divine judgment.

The concept of universal history which is at work in hermeneutics should be thought of as a "fore-understanding," a provisional and anticipatory projection of the ultimate truth of history.[25] It is thus a heuristic device, but not just that. The interpreter holds his or her concept of universal history as a truth, though again as a truth which must be tested with the passing of time.

The specific ideas which seem to lie at the heart of Pannenberg's concept of universal history are (1) the traditional notion that God is directing history to its completion, and (2) the notion that a prolepsis of the Kingdom has been given through Jesus of Nazareth (themes that will be explored in subsequent chapters). In this regard, he makes use of Dilthey's claim that the meaning of the historical process as a whole could be ascertained only from the standpoint of its end.[26] Since no one in fact stands at the end, Dilthey concluded from this consideration that the truth of history is simply not to be found. In his novel appropriation of the insight, however, Pannenberg comes to a different conclusion. He allows that it is only the end which can provide the truth of the whole; but the view of universal history as an anticipation of the end is relevant precisely at this point. "Every assertion of meaning rests upon a fore-conception (Vorgriff) of the final future, in the light of which the true meaning of every individual event first becomes expressible in a valid way."[27] More particularly, the Christian interpreter views any event within the historical process from the standpoint of a view of universal history which is grounded in the anticipation of

34

the truth of the whole revealed in the life,
death, and especially the Resurrection of Jesus.

At this point, we should pause to consider
a rather obvious question. Pannenberg begins
with a contextual theory of meaning and truth
and ends with a view of universal history. These
two ideas are not easily meshed. Indeed, at
first glance they seem to be contradictory. If
an ultimate context is available after all, then
why all the bother about the conceptual distance
between different historical contexts?

To answer this question, we should note
the carefully qualified character of Pannenberg's
comments on the idea of universal history. He
always speaks of such as "provisional," "anticipatory," and "hypothetical." There is nothing
final about any particular interpreter's concept
of universal history. Pannenberg allows, in
fact, that one's concept of universal history is
itself conditioned by historical circumstances
and is thus context-bound.[28] Hence, in answer
to the question, we can say that an ultimate
and absolute context is not really <u>available</u>.
The various interpreters have only time-bound
anticipations regarding such a context.

It should be pointed out, however, that
the various concepts of universal history are
concepts <u>of</u> an ultimate and definitive context.
Pannenberg holds that with the completion of the
historical process an absolute and final context
of meaning and truth will be established in fact.[29]
And it is important to understand that this context will not be subject to change because there
will be no further historical development in
which it could be changed. It will be established by an act of God once and for all. And
furthermore, according to Pannenberg, the truth
which becomes evident in that broadest of all
contexts will be the retroactive measure of all
historical truth-claims.[30] In other words, when
the <u>eschaton</u> comes, universal history will be

35

complete; and the truth unveiled at the eschaton
is the absolute truth for all historical contexts.

Thus, when we talk not about the various
temporal conceptions of universal history but
about universal history itself, it is evident
that Pannenberg's position is not finally that
of a relativist. He believes, when all is said
and done, in one absolute standard for truth.
This may appear to violate the spirit of his contextualism, but it does not in fact. Pannenberg
is consistently contextualistic and relativistic
so far as any given set of beliefs is concerned
at some particular point in the process. That
is, on the presuppositions of his theory, no one
could claim that any particular set of religious
beliefs is in fact the absolute truth of history.
One could only claim that there is, or perhaps
better, there will be, an ultimate religious
truth. In this way, the integrity of the differing historical contexts is preserved.

With the addition of the concept of universal history as an ultimate context, all of the
essential ingredients of Pannenberg's particular
kind of contextualism are now before us. Keeping
this general theory of meaning and truth in the
background, let us turn to his work on the age-
old problem of analogy.

Analogy, Context, and Verifiability

The doctrine of analogy, it should be recalled, was designed to provide a 'middle way'
in regard to speech about God. On the one hand,
it was set over against the view that terms
which ordinarily apply to creatures may be
applied univocally to God. This view, it was
thought, did not do justice to the transcendence
of God. And on the other hand, it was set over
against the view that terms which ordinarily
apply to creatures may only be applied in an

36

equivocal way to God. This view, it was thought, did not do justice to the possibility of human knowledge of God.

According to the Thomistic tradition, there are basically two types of analogy which are important theologically--the analogy of attribution and the analogy of proper proportionality. In brief, according to the analogy of attribution, certain characteristics are said to apply both to human beings and to God but to belong 'properly' only to God. For instance, we can say that both God and human beings are good. This characteristic is proper, or natural, to the being of God. But the human being, in contrast, is good only in the derivative sense that he or she as a creature of God receives a share of the divine goodness.

In the analogy of proper proportionality, a parallel is said to exist between the way in which a certain characteristic is related to the being of a creature and the way in which a similar characteristic is related to the being of the Creator. In this case, both analogates are thought to possess the characteristic properly. Using goodness as the example once again, we can say that both God and human beings are quite literally good. The two analogates differ, however, in that each possesses the characteristic 'proportionately' to the kind of being involved. That is, the being of the human is finite, so his or her goodness is the goodness proper to a finite being. And the being of God is infinite, so the divine goodness is the goodness proper to an infinite being. The analogy in regard to goodness, then, would be expressed in this case in the following way: As the goodness of the human is to the being of the human, so the goodness of God is to the being of God.[31]

Pannenberg raises numerous objections to the classical doctrine of analogy, especially the analogy of proper proportionality. For our purposes, the most interesting of these is his claim that there simply is <u>no middle ground</u> between univocity and equivocity. As he sees it, analogy is not an "independent third" type of usage, but a "mere mixture" of univocal and equivocal predication. Furthermore, if analogy is a mere mixture, then there remains in every analogy an irreducible element of univocity. There is always, as he puts it, an "identical logos" which "makes the analogates analogous."[32]

Pannenberg attacks the doctrine of analogy in his article, "Analogy and Doxology." Though it is not spelled out in the article, he must presuppose something like the following for his argument regarding the identical logos.[33] He must want to force the issue by asking whether the relations involved are identical or only similar. In either case, he will argue, a univocal core is present.[34] If we say that the goodness of the human is to the being of the human <u>as</u> the goodness of God is to the being of God, what does the 'as' mean? Does it mean 'exactly alike' or only 'somewhat alike'? If it is the latter, then Pannenberg wants to know in <u>what</u> respects the relations are alike, and in <u>what</u> respects they are different. When this question is answered, he will have the univocal core. If it is the former, that is, if the 'as' means 'exactly alike', then he already has the element of univocity.

I am not concerned here to respond directly to Pannenberg's criticism of the doctrine of analogy. My purpose, rather, is to show what his criticism implies for his general position on theological language. On the assumption that analogy always has a univocal core, he rejects the doctrine as inconsistent with the transcendent God of theism. Pannenberg speaks in this regard of the "spiritual violence," or "spiritual assault," which occurs in the traditional concept of analogy.[35] The doctrine, he says, presupposes

"an attitude which is certainly inappropriate
with respect to God."[36] Further, once we become
aware of the univocity buried in analogy, "it
is no longer possible to overlook its contra-
diction to the intention of adoration and devo-
tion which is alone appropriate for a legitimate
knowledge of God."[37]

Pannenberg puts in contrast to the concept
of analogy an idea of theological language as
"doxology," a notion developed by Edmund Schlink,
in his work, The Coming Christ and the Coming
Church. The term is derived from the Greek doxa,
which in New Testament usage means "glory." Doxological speech is thus essentially praise of, or
adoration for God. It keeps in the forefront,
according to Pannenberg, the transcendent otherness of God, and the corresponding need for hu-
mility upon the part of human beings.[38]

From the tag "doxology," it sounds as
though he is speaking of a language of worship
which is essentially performative in function.
But this is decidedly not the case. Doxological
language, Pannenberg affirms, consists of assertions about God, not just prayer or praise
directed to God.[39] At the same time, however,
he says openly and without qualification that
the language used in doxology is equivocal in
character. In speaking of God, the believer
"sacrifices" himself or herself in the act of
speaking by releasing the words from the "mani-
pulation" of the thinker. Such is accomplished,
Pannenberg maintains, specifically through one's
willingness to admit a discontinuity between the
ordinary meaning of the term employed and its
meaning when transferred to God.[40]

> The creaturely content of our concepts is
> sacrificed when goodness, righteousness, love,
> wisdom, etc., are ascribed to the eternal
> essence of God. This means, with regard to
> the concepts themselves, that they become
> equivocal in the act of transferring their

their finite contents to the eternal essence
of God.[41]

The motivation for Pannenberg's view of
theological language as doxological is not hard
to find. He is rather obviously seeking in this
regard to accommodate Barth, Bultmann, and the
dialectical theology which has been so dominant
in the twentieth century. In this conception,
God is thought to be "wholly other," and any
view of language which accepts the doctrine of
analogy is thought to compromise the otherness
of God, to reduce the divine to the level of
human constructs. Pannenberg's rejection of
analogy goes hand in glove with the approach of
dialectical theology, and his acceptance of the
view that theological language is basically doxological seems even to be an effort to carry that
tradition forward.

It seems to me, however, that the frank
acceptance of equivocity tends to undermine Pannenberg's otherwise thoughtful and well-developed
theory of meaning and truth. To say that theological terms are equivocal in reference to God
is, as Pannenberg sees, to say that we do not
know what they mean in such reference. And if
we take seriously the admission of ignorance in
this regard, it becomes questionable why we are
willing to use certain terms, such as 'good',
'loving', and 'just', of God rather than others,
such as 'bad', 'hateful', and 'unjust'.

This point may be clarified by reference to
one way in which theists sometimes attempt to
exonerate God from the charge that the divine
being is evil. It is occasionally argued that
what appears to be unjust from our finite perspective (the suffering of infants, etc.) might
actually be just from the divine, infinite perspective, and that our complaints about the
suffering of the innocent may in this way simply
reveal our ignorance. That may be. But it is

40

important to see also that if this particular kind of theodicy is used, common value terms such as 'just' immediately lost their meaning when applied to God, and it no longer makes any sense to say that God is either just or unjust.

Pannenberg's 'doxology' is beset by the same problem. If terms such as 'good', 'loving', and 'just', are equivocal in reference to God and humanity, then our use of them in regard to God has essentially no meaning. In fact, it becomes impossible to erect any kind of criterion which could serve to distinguish terms that might properly be used of God and those that could not be so employed. In this case, it might be best not to say anything about God at all, in other words, to become a mystic on the one side or an agnostic on the other.

It may be that Pannenberg's approach to the question of analogy represents only a tendency toward overstatement, a characteristic which was apparent also in the earlier discussion of the historicity of truth. There, it might be recalled, he used terminology which was, in the final analysis, somewhat misleading. If there is, after all, an absolute truth for universal history, then truth is not finally historical. By the same token, it may be that here he gives lip-service to a position which is really inconsistent with his view of theological language in general and which he really does not want to hold. If not, there seems to be a significant point of tension in his view of theological language as a whole.

The problem can be made especially clear by reference to Pannenberg's endorsement of John Hick's notion of eschatological verification. In his <u>Philosophy of Religion</u>, Hick argues that theism makes factual claims about the world, and especially about the destiny of humanity. The universe envisaged by the theist thus differs markedly from that envisaged by the nontheist.

41

Though there is not at present a means of verifying the theist's claims, if the theist is right, the end of history will allow for verification. According to Hick, the situation with respect to verification is like that of two travelers who argue about the destination at the end of the road. They make rival claims, and put forward some conflicting data in support of the hypotheses; but it is only at the end of the journey that they will see who was right.[42] Pannenberg argues in a similar way:

> Only the end of all history can bring the final decision about assertions in respect to reality as a whole, and thus also in respect to the reality of God and the determination of mankind.[43]

Unfortunately, according to Pannenberg's program, eschatological verification seems really to be an impossibility. It would seem that a necessary condition for the possibility of verification of a statement is that those who seek to verify it know what it means. If they do not, then obviously they will have no idea as to what state of affairs might serve to verify or falsify the claim. If Pannenberg's equivocity is taken for what it says, then there is no way for us, or anyone else, to know what a statement about God means, and hence there is no way in which such a statement might be evaluated.

Sometimes the concept of verifiability is spelled out in such a way that the specification of the conditions under which a statement might be verified constitutes itself the meaning of the statement. Thus it might be argued on behalf of Pannenberg that the conditions which hold in the projected eschaton, since they are construed as verifying conditions, constitute the meaning of the statements which one might wish to make about God or the destiny of humanity. This is a plausible line of defense, but if it is taken, then it is no longer possible to defend equivocity because the meanings of the terms employed are specified in the verifying conditions themselves.

My point is really quite simple. If Pannenberg wants to accept eschatological verification, then he should, it seems, give up equivocity. And if he wants to accept the latter, then no program of verification for theological statements, including of course eschatological verification, is useful.

This criticism by no means serves to call into question, however, his work on the meaning and truth of theological language in general. I do not see why Pannenberg could not accept analogy instead of equivocity. Indeed, it appears to me that his general contextual theory requires a doctrine of analogy.

The approach which Pannenberg has developed is obviously designed to be a mean between the religious extremes of dogmatism and skepticism. It is a carefully-reasoned position which allows that theological claims should be taken seriously but also tentatively. They should be neither absolutized nor trivialized. We have at any given time an anticipatory projection to make about the ultimate meaning of all reality, a projection which will be confirmed or disconfirmed at the eschaton.

As we noted at the beginning of this section, however, the doctrine of analogy was designed in reality for the very same purposes. Analogy represents the mean between the extremes of equivocity and univocity. Pannenberg's provisional theological knowledge is best construed as the modern counterpart to analogy, not a rejection of it. His approach represents the same compromise as analogy has represented in the Thomistic tradition, though now the compromise is worked out in terms of epistemology and the philosophy of science rather than metaphysics

43

and Aristotelian logic. I suggest, then, that
the 'middle way' is exactly what Pannenberg has
been putting forth in the context of twentieth-
century theological and philosophical concerns,
and as such it represents a significant contribution to contemporary religious philosophy.

In response to Pannenberg's argument
against the doctrine, it should be pointed out
that the concept of analogical language really
does not sacrifice the divine otherness as dialectical theologians have insisted generally.
To say that terms which we use of God have a
meaning in some ways similar to and in some ways
dissimilar to their ordinary meanings is but
another way of saying that we can claim no dogmatic certainty in reference to theology. We
think, we believe, we project, we claim tentative
knowledge, but we cannot claim to know in full
at this point. This willingness to forego the
claim to certainty in theological knowledge preserves the otherness of God. And it is this
which is really at the heart of the doctrine of
analogy and Pannenberg's hermeneutics.

In conclusion, though there are problems
in Pannenberg's contextual theory of theological
language, it seems to me that he makes important
contributions to modern religious philosophy in
this connection. By calling attention to the
context-boundedness of theological statements,
and at the same time the cultural and historical
variability of theological beliefs, Pannenberg
opens the door from the theistic standpoint to
an appreciation for the integrity and significance of the religious experience of non-
Christians. In this respect, he corrects the
extreme assertions of dialectical theology to
the effect that there is a single, absolute, and
exclusive revelation of God in Christ. In itself, of course, an appreciation for non-
Christian religions is nothing new in religious
philosophy. The significance of Pannenberg's
work is that his approach makes it possible for

Protestant theologians, with their strong biblical orientation, to participate in philosophical discussions once again. In contrast, the approach of dialectical theology tended to isolate and even insulate the Protestant tradition from philosophical analysis.

In addition, Pannenberg's contribution at this point serves to bring together several currents of thought in the modern world. In effect, he unites historical theology, religious philosophy of the analytic sort with its concern for language and verification, and the historicism which is such a strong current in contemporary European philosophy. Often the study of the philosophy of religion is carried out in an arid fashion, abstracted from cultural and even theological concerns. An approach to theological language such as Pannenberg's helps to correct that tendency.

And finally, despite the point of tension between his positions on the question of analogy and the question of meaning and truth in general, Pannenberg's work on language points to a way in which to make contemporary the insight of the ancient doctrine of analogy. His notion of theological claims as significant on the one hand but provisional on the other hand seems to be a modern counterpart to the 'middle way' of analogy. It seems, in his own way of speaking, to be a moment in the history of the transmission of the same tradition.

[1]TPS, pp. 206-11.   [2]Ibid., p. 212.

[3]Ibid., p. 182.

[4]Schubert Ogden's book, Christ Without Myth (New York: Harper and Brothers, 1961), pp. 95-126, is especially helpful at this point. The crucial material in the Bultmann corpus, in my opinion, is found in his essay, "What Does it Mean to Speak of God?" in Faith and Understanding (New York: Harper and Row, 1969), pp. 53-65. Here he denies altogether that it is meaningful to speak of God without "self-reference." But if reference to God must always include reference to self, it is logically impossible to separate God from the selves of various speakers.

[5]"Hermeneutic and Universal History," in BQT, 1:109.

[6]Ibid., pp. 109-10.   [7]Ibid., p. 109.

[8]Ibid., p. 111.

[9]Ibid., pp. 111-13, quote p. 113.

[10]This theme is ubiquitous in the work of Bultmann. It is especially obvious, of course, in his programmatic essay, "New Testament and Mythology," in Kerygma and Myth, ed. Hans-Werner Bartsch, trans. Reginald H. Fuller, 2 vols. (London: SPCK, 1953-62), 1:1-44.

[11]"What is Truth?" in BQT, 2:20.

[12]Ibid., p. 21.   [13]Ibid., p. 20.

[14]Ibid., pp. 20-21.

[15]This is obvious throughout TPS, but especially so in his discussion of the Popper-Kuhn controversy and in his development of the history of hermeneutics during the past century. See TPS, pp. 35-58, 156-224.

[16]Ibid., p. 41, n. 62.

[17]"Hermeneutic and Universal History," p. 117. Gadamer puts forward the idea of a fusion of horizons in his work, Truth and Method, trans. and ed. Garrett Barden and John Cumming (New York: Seabury Press, 1975), pp. 267-74.

[18]Gadamer, Truth and Method, p. 269.

[19]Ibid., p. 273.   [20]Ibid., p. 268.

[21]Ibid., p. 270.   [22]TPS, p. 198.

[23]"Hermeneutic and Universal History," p. 129. In an ingenious argument, Pannenberg even attempts to show that Christianity has been largely determinative for contemporary hermeneutics in that the basic model which must be assumed for hermeneutical endeavor was historically supplied precisely by the Christian faith. Ted Peters, in his article, "Truth in History: Gadamer's Hermeneutics and Pannenberg's Apologetic Method," The Journal of Religion 55 (January 1975):36-56, provides an excellent summary of the argument.

[24]"Hermeneutic and Universal History," pp. 129-30.

[25]TPS, p. 201.

[26]Wilhelm Dilthey, Pattern and Meaning in History, ed. H. P. Rickman (London: Allen and Unwin, 19610, p. 100. For Pannenberg's discussion, see "Faith and Reason," pp. 61-62.

47

[27]"Faith and Reason," p. 62.

[28]TPS, p. 201. Frank Tupper makes a similar point regarding Pannenberg's view of the universality of church doctrine, or dogmatics:

> Dogmatics must continually accomplish a
> new and contemporary explication of the
> universal meaning of the transmitted tra-
> dition, because the historic expressions
> of the universal truth of the Christ event
> are conditioned by time and culture (Tupper,
> The Theology of Wolfhart Pannenberg, p. 68).

[29]"Future and Unity," in Hope and the Future of Man, ed. Ewert H. Cousins (Philadelphia: Fortress Press, 1972), p. 73.

[30]TKG, p. 63.

[31]There are many passages in the corpus of St. Thomas which stand behind this summary statement of the doctrine. Most important are two passages from De veritate: Q. 11, Art. 2, and Q. 21, Art. 4. I have found James Anderson's discussions of analogy in his work, Reflections on the Analogy of Being (The Hague: Martinus Nijhoff, 1967, to be particularly illuminating in regard to the analogy of proper proportionality.

[32]"Analogy and Doxology," in BQT, 1:224.

[33]In the article, "Analogy and Doxology," Pannenberg refers to his inaugural dissertation, "Analogie und Offenbarung" (Heidelberg, 1955), for the actual argumentation in support of this stand. So far as I know, this essay remains unpublished. I rely strictly on the article and the general tenor of Pannenberg's thought for this construction.

[34]"Analogy and Doxology," p. 222, n. 18. He criticizes St. Thomas, for instance, for overlooking the univocal core in the relations.

[35]Ibid., pp. 224-25.   [36]Ibid., p. 224.

[37]Ibid., p. 225.   [38]Ibid., pp. 215-17.

[39]"What is a Dogmatic Statement?" in BQT, 1:202-3.

[40]Ibid., pp. 203-4; also, "Analogy and Doxology," pp. 215-17.

[41]"What is a Dogmatic Statement?" p. 203.

[42]John Hick, Philosophy of Religion (Englewood Cliffs, N. J.: Prentice-Hall, 1963), pp. 100-101.

[43]TPS, p. 343. My translation differs slightly. It depends on the original German in Wissenschaftstheorie und Theologie (Frankfurt am Main: Suhrkamp Verlag, 1973), p. 347.

Chapter Three

THEOLOGY AS A SCIENCE

Pannenberg has written on an enormous number of theological questions, but one of his most
abiding concerns has been the general conception
of the task of theology itself. He raises openly
and honestly the question which should be faced
by every theologian in our time, 'What is the
theological project?' Generally speaking, Pannenberg argues that theology should be conceived
as a science, more specifically, a science of
God. In this chapter, I outline the picture of
theology as a science which is emerging from his
work, and then offer a brief critique of his
program.

A Science of God

The topic was first approached by Pannenberg in his essay, "Toward a Theology of the History of Religions" (first published, 1967);[1] and
he amplifies the original proposal in his more recent work, Theology and the Philosophy of Science.

To begin with, he maintains in the early
essay that Christianity must no longer be given
a special category as "revelation" over against
the general category of "religion" as was done
in the dialectical theology of Barth and Bultmann. Rather, it must be seen "as a religion
among the religions."[2] If theology hopes to be
taken seriously outside its own community, he
says, then it must appeal to the facts of the
history of religions, not just to its own presuppositions.[3] He allows that theology should
not deny its generally "Christian perspective,"
and could scarcely be accomplished "without commitment to the God of the Bible."[4] At the same
time, however, it should not use its Christian

51

presuppositions in the course of argumentation.[5] That these last two points are in tension did not escape his notice. And in Theology and the Philosophy of Science he clarifies his position, saying now that the scholars who conduct theological inquiry need not be Christian, and that if they are in fact, their Christianity will be of service only in the order of discovery, not the order of justification.[6]

Pannenberg is very careful to distinguish his program from what has come to be known as the 'phenomenology of religion', from Hegel's approach to religions, and from the ordinary history of religions courses offered in many universities. He criticizes the phenomenological approach for its overemphasis on types of religious experience and cross-cultural similarities. It detaches, he says, the forms in which religious life finds expression from the actual historical contexts of the expression.[7] Since it abstracts from historical particularity, it is unable to grasp in a rigorous empirical fashion either the uniqueness of the various religious traditions or the historical development of such.[8] He brings the similar charge against Hegel that the latter regarded the particular religions as types through which consciousness passes en route to self-realization. "There was hardly a word in Hegel about the history of religions themselves."[9] And on the other side, the popular history of religions courses in universities contain ample detail in relation to the actual development of religions, but they do not consider the question of the truth of religions. The program which Pannenberg envisages does not "bracket out" the question of the "reality-reference" (Wirklichkeitsbezug) embodied in religious claims.[10] Despite its strong empirical orientation, this study is after all a theology. As such its object in attending to the history of religions is precisely the "reality of God."[11]

In Theology and the Philosophy of Science,
Pannenberg refers to theology as a "science of
God."[12] The idea of God is, of course, problematic for the modern world. It can no longer
be taken for granted that God exists, or that
God is revealed ultimately in Christ. At the
same time, however, neither should it be taken
for granted, as is sometimes done from the standpoint of the projection theory, that God does not
exist. A sounder view is that the question of
God is open and unsettled. Hence, if theology
is a science of God, the latter must be its object precisely as a problem as well as a point
of reference for its inquiry.[13]

Since God is not one object among others
in our empirical experience, how can there be a
science of God? It is possible, Pannenberg argues, on the assumption that the reality of God
is given with the experience of other objects,
or, in other words, that God is indirectly revealed through our various human experiences of
reality. This is not to say that there is no
direct experience of God. Indeed, the very
heart of the religious consciousness through the
centuries has been the direct encounter. But,
such encounters have only subjective significance. They obtain intersubjective significance
only by being brought to thematic expression,
that is, by being made relevant to human self-
understanding and our general understanding of
the world. In this way, the experience of God
as the object of theology is always indirect;
it is mediated through the linguistic community
of the tradition in the context of which it
occurs.[14]

If the reality of God is to be discovered
through the experience of other objects, just
which objects should be the focus of theological
inquiry? Pannenberg's unequivocal answer is that
it should be focused on all objects. Taking his
cue from Bultmann's article, "What Does it Mean

53

to Speak of God?"[15] he thinks of God as "the
Reality that determines everything" (die alles-
bestimmende Wirklichkeit). The monotheistic
traditions, he points out, have been characterized throughout their histories by the assertion
that the power that stands behind everything
which we experience is one, and that it is this
power which provides for the unity of the universe.[16] And the assertion that one unified
power stands behind everything implies that
every object "should be shown to be a trace of
the divine reality."[17] This is not to say that
each thing as an isolated individual should be
taken up into theological inquiry; rather, such
inquiry should be focused on objects in their
interconnections with each other and their places
in the whole scheme of things. Hence, according
to Pannenberg, the theologian has the whole of
reality as his or her domain of objects; and
the guiding question is whether the reality of
God can be shown to be the uniting power behind
everything.

At first glance, such a project seems obviously objectionable. Kant pointed out that
just as God is not given as an object of human
experience, neither is the whole of reality.
Again, then, we must ask how theologians can
do their work. Here Pannenberg invokes what is
virtually a standard formula for his approach to
the various questions at issue in the discussion
and his approach to religious philosophy in
general: "The totality of reality is not conclusively present. It is only anticipated as a
totality of meaning."[18] And the loci of these
anticipations, in their most profound and concrete expressions, are the historical religions.
So, theology should look first to the actual
religious traditions for their anticipations of
a totality of meaning, anticipations which attempt to embody the whole of reality, the latter
being the domain of objects through which the
power of God, the proper object of theology, is
expressed.[19]

Pannenberg has a very exciting appreciation
for the importance of the varied religious traditions. Often as not, philosophers of religion
carry out their inquiry in abstraction from considerations pertaining to the concrete religions.
The existence and attributes of God, miracles,
and the afterlife are discussed as though these
concepts could be removed from the religious traditions in which they arose. Pannenberg is rejecting this tendency as shortsighted. It is,
in his opinion, the historical orientation of
theology which actually provides its scientific
character. The reality of God, he argues, is
present in historical models, which means that
they are "subject to confirmation or refutation
by subsequent experience."20

Theology as a science of God, then, is
really a science of religion, and not of religion in general, but of the historical religions.21
Thus, Christian theology is a science of the
Christian religion, and by implication Islamic
theology is a science of the Islamic religion,
etc. The task of the theology of any particular
religion is to make the projections of meaning
within it explicit. And theology in general is
the critical, comparative study of the various
religions with the basic question in view of how
well they preserve unity amid the diversity of
human experience.22

Confirmation in Theology

The possibility of "confirmation or refutation" is crucial for any kind of inquiry which
would go under the name of science, even in the
loose, German sense of Wissenschaft. "Science"
as Pannenberg uses it, and as is typical of German usage, includes on the one side the Natur-
wissenschaften, the natural sciences as every-
where understood, and on the other side the

55

Geivteswissenschaften, sciences which have to do
with questions related to human existence in
its various contexts. In this latter category
are included among others sociology, psychology,
anthropology, history, philosophy, and in Pannenberg's view, at least, even theology.

The thrust of his theological and philosophical work from the beginning has been to re-
ject the reduction of theological truth-claims
to subjective projections whose truth is available only to the "eyes of faith." In his work
on the concept of the scientific character of
theology, that concern is especially obvious.
He does not believe that the Geisteswissenschaften
are subjective in methodology whereas the Natur-
wissenschaften are objective. Though he appropriates some of Gadamer's insights, as we have
seen, he criticizes the latter's refusal to allow
for the "constitutive importance of the statement as the expression of the representational
function of language."[23] Gadamer in effect rejects the "objectifying function" of language;
he does not account for the way in which the
speaker distinguishes the content of the assertion from his or her own subjectivity.[24] If we
allow for the crucial role of the assertion even
in the Geisteswissenschaften, and note that to
assert is to objectify in the sense above, it
becomes arbitrary to distinguish history, philosophy, and theology from the natural sciences by
reference to the objective/subjective distinction.

Specifically in relation to the objectivity
of theology, Pannenberg argues that theological
utterances also have the character of assertion,
and that theologians should accept the implications of this fact. One of these implications
is that what is spoken about must be distin-
guishable from the assertions of believers and
theologians about it. Pannenberg holds that if
the reality of God cannot be so distinguished
from assertions of faith about it, "such assertions can no longer be taken seriously as

assertions, but look like fictions created by believers and theologians."[25]

Furthermore, a corollary of the distinction between the subjectivity of the speaker and the objectivity of his or her statement is that statements must in some way be <u>testable</u> (though not necessarily by the criterion of direct empirical observation).[26] Pannenberg makes his position quite clear in this respect. "Theology must not avoid the demand for a means of testing its statements by criteria other than those of an authoritative doctrinal tradition."[27] The testing procedure, in other words, must not be bound from the beginning to the subjectivity of the theologian's tradition, but must allow for intersubjective assessment.

Pannenberg maintains that the positivist's requirement of verifiability or falsifiability by direct empirical observation cannot even be met in the natural science.[28] But the statements made therein do, of course, have objective significance. They make claims about states of affairs which can be checked through the relevant testing procedures of the given scientific community with its ruling paradigms and language assumptions. The objectivity of the natural sciences which Pannenberg wishes to link with the the human sciences, and even theology, is directly tied to this notion of a test which can be administered independently of the biases of the scientists involved.[29]

So, what is the test to which theological claims must be put? He has described the criterion in a variety of ways. Basically, however, it seems to be the test of comprehensiveness. In the essay, "Toward a Theology of the History of Religions," for instance, he says:

The need for an encompassing unity that makes it possible to experience even the

multifarious as a positive wealth is so
deeply rooted in human existence and in
the structure of human reason that it
inevitably brings up the question of the
extent to which this religion or that can
provide a basis for a universal unity in
the experience of reality, which is very
likely the criterion of its relevance and
saving power--and thus, perhaps, of its
truth, too.[30]

And a similar idea is expressed in Theology and
the Philosophy of Science:

The theologian for his part can formulate
hypotheses which are related to the distinctive order (Rang) of religions, of
the superiority of one religion's tradition
over that of others in respect to their
anticipatory comprehension of reality as
a whole and thus as a self-manifestation
of God.[31]

It is important to have a clear understanding of the test since so much, in terms of
whether theology can really be a science, seems
to depend on it. Some additional descriptions
should help to fill out the general concept of
comprehensiveness. In his recent little theological work, Human Nature, Election, and History (1977), Pannenberg addresses the issue of
a criterion for answering the question whether
God exists in the following way:

In my opinion, such a criterion can be
found in the illuminative power of a given
idea of God. The criterion is applied when
we ask how a particular idea of God illuminates and has illuminated our understanding
of reality and, especially, of human life.[32]

In many places, he associates this illuminative
power specifically with our contemporary experience of reality. For instance, in the article,

58

"The Nature of a Theological Statement," he explains the test in this way: "Statements about God can be examined as to whether their content is really of determinative significance for all finite reality as it is available to our experience" (my emphasis).33 And the discussion in Theology and the Philosophy of Science contains the same suggestion. The question, he says, is how far a particular religious tradition "in fact takes account of all the currently accessible aspects of reality."34 And further, "The traditional claims of a religion may therefore be regarded as hypotheses to be tested by the full range of currently accessible experience."35

One additional element must be added. Since in the modern world there has been a decidedly anthropological turn, especially in philosophy, it is no longer possible to ascertain the significance of the idea of God directly in relation to the world, as was done, for example, by natural theology in its cosmological and teleological arguments. Rather, our access to the significance of the God-idea comes only through inquiry into "man's self-understanding and his relation to the world."36

Collecting the various points of emphasis exhibited in these quotes, we can say that the test involves the comprehensive power of a religious tradition specifically in respect to how well it illuminates our present experience of reality, with the latter's human orientation, by providing in an anticipatory way a sense of wholeness or unity in that experience. The procedure, or criterion, seems to involve a kind of correlation in which there is on the one side the particular idea of God as developed in a given religious tradition and on the other side there is the modern experience of reality as a whole. And theology as a science of God, and hence of the historical religions, is the comparative investigation of this correlation with the purpose of showing that one or another

59

of the traditions preserves a sense of unity
better than the others.

The correlation has basically two aspects,
and these two aspects themselves correspond to
the two kinds of associations which one must make
in an analysis of the testability of theological
claims. The correlation involves first a historical aspect. As we noted in the last chapter,
in Pannenberg's view the theologian's hermeneutical project is to appropriate critically his or
her tradition in such a way as to make contact
with the modern world, though not in such a way
as to accept the assumptions of modernity in
toto as a criterion for the truth of the tradition. The project is critical both in respect
to the tradition and in respect to modernity.
It is not to judge the tradition by modern assumptions, but to see if the tradition, critically received, can provide a basis for, or as
we have noted above, can illuminate the modern
experience. To do the interpretative work described, one must begin with the appropriation
of the tradition itself.

In this regard, theological claims are
like historical claims in general, and must
be evaluated by the same criteria which are
applicable to the latter. Such claims often
relate to the events that are central to the
given tradition and the history of the interpretation of those events. They differ from
straightforward historical claims in that theology is not interested in establishing simply
the factuality of the past event but rather
the appearance of God in it and thus its significance for our modern experience.[37] This is
not a matter of "seeing as," however, according
to which a secular historian would see an isolated historical event and the theologian would
see the same event as an act of God. Such an
approach would excuse the historical theologian
from the rigorous requirements involved in the
confirmation of historical hypotheses. The

historical theologian, like the secular historian, should provide the requisite historical evidence for whatever claims he or she wishes to make about the transmission of the tradition or any of the events recorded within it.

Though the similarity with historical statements is important to Pannenberg's position on the scientific character of theology, for the most part I shall reserve discussion of this aspect of the position for the chapter on the Resurrection. There is, however, one implication of the historical nature of many theological claims which deserves more pointed attention in this context. It seems to me that Pannenberg is suggesting that one of the tests for a theological claim is just the question how well it makes contact with the very tradition from which it supposedly comes. This hearkens back in another way to the concern with hermeneutics. Interpretation always involves critical appropriation, but it is, after all, appropriation. A theological claim that can show no contact with the tradition (of Christianity or others) would already be suspect, Pannenberg is saying.

The correlation involves secondly a philosophical aspect, and this will be the focus of my concern. Since on one side of the correlation there is the modern experience of reality, and since one of the tasks of philosophy, as Pannenberg sees it, is to synthesize and bring to thematic expression the various relations of meaning which run throughout the diverse fields of human inquiry, theological statements resemble philosophical statements in regard to the intent to provide for the unity of experience.[38] In the light of this parallel, Pannenberg suggests that theological statements are subject to the same criteria as are utterances of a philosophical sort. The criteria in this case are again related to integration and comprehension.

61

To the extent that a philosophical model integrates the areas of experience already worked out in the sciences with each other and with the areas of prescientific experience, it substantiates its claim to describe the still open totality of meaning of experience.[39]

The philosophical side of the project itself seems to have two divisions, though this is not made explicit by Pannenberg. On one side, there is the theological task within the hermeneutical community of any tradition of showing how the distinctive historical doctrines of that tradition actually illumine the problems and concerns of modern experience; and on the other side, there is the intertraditional comparative analysis whereby the argument is made that one tradition better accomodates the modern experience than others.

In regard to the former--the illuminative hermeneutical project--Pannenberg by any standard has to be deemed a brilliant success. There are numerous distinctive commitments which he associates with the modern understanding of reality. Prominent among these are the ideas (1) that reality is historical, (2) that the future is open, and (3) that the human being has the freedom of Weltoffenheit, the capacity always to negate, or transcend the present in the light of new possibilities for the future.[40] On each of these commitments, as well as on many other prevalent themes of the modern understanding, Pannenberg does painstakingly-detailed work in the effort to show how the modern understanding was influenced by the Christian tradition, and further how certain aspects of the tradition which have been sedimented, or covered over, in modernity shed considerable light on our own conceptual impasses. I shall take up his work on the significance of the Resurrection and the Christian ideas of God and freedom in the next two chapters, and I shall postpone for the present final judgment on the success of the details of his approach in these areas. Suffice it to say here that Pannenberg has had considerable success in this distinctively hermeneutical undertaking.

In regard to the comparative project outlined above, however, it is not so obvious that Pannenberg's program is either sound conceptually or successful in application. Before an informed critique of this aspect of the testing procedure can be developed, however, two very important qualifications should be noted.

First, Pannenberg points out that no theological statement can be confirmed by itself. Like statements in other fields of science, theological claims must be evaluated in connection with the general theories in which they occur.[41] He means by this qualification that individual theological claims must be considered together with the other basic claims which are implicit in the particular tradition under consideration. In regard to the traditional problem of evil, for instance, the claim might be 'God is good'. The presence of natural evil in the world could count strongly against that claim taken by itself. But when linked with other aspects of the tradition, such as 'Without suffering, there can be no salvation', and 'God will ultimately redeem the whole creation', the original claim is not damaged so extensively by the presence of evil.

The second qualification which Pannenberg attaches to his procedure is the admission that there is no conclusive test for theological statements, at least in our historical experience, just as there is no conclusive test for statements in the other fields of science. He allows, however, that the difficulties in this regard are exacerbated for theology due to the facts that the claims are so large and the whole of reality to which they refer is not available.

We stand in the middle of the historical process; and our understanding of reality is always subject to change. Hence, as was pointed out in the preceding chapter, our assessment of the truth value of religious claims is always tentative at best.[42]

With these qualifications, I believe that the salient points in the distinctively philosophical aspect of Pannenberg's testing procedure are now before us. The general idea of a correlation between theological claims and the modern experience of reality seems reasonably clear. Having stated the procedure in some detail, let us ask what might be the result of its deployment.

Difficulties in Pannenberg's Approach

In the first place, there is an immediate problem for those who have been influenced by the analytic school of philosophy, of course, and that is the doubt whether even philosophy can perform the synthetic task described above, much less theology. Especially acute in this regard is the notorious lack of uniformity in the modern experience of reality. In the modern philosophical community alone, there are Marxists, positivists, existentialists, Thomists, linguistic analysts, process philosophers, and bushels-full of scholars whose commitments represent an overlapping of these or still some further set of basic presuppositions. The modern experience is, in short, pluralistic. And to nail down exactly which commitments in fact characterize in the most general sense the modern experience seems impossible, unless it is to say only that we moderns are pluralistic itself.

I have no doubt that Pannenberg is fully aware of this complexity. Indeed, in places he

even attempts to relate the Christian tradition
specifically to pluralism. But I do not see how
his program for testing theological claims circumvents the problems arising from the pluralistic
character of contemporary philosophical commitments. The correlation described above requires
at least a loosely-definable set of modern commitments; in actuality, the prominent characteristics of modern thought which are generally
endorsed by Pannenberg represent only one way
of assessing the contemporary philosophical
scene, or in other words, only one among several
possible sets of commitments.

      In the second place, one gets the feeling
that in regard to the comparative project the deck
is stacked. Christianity has obviously been a
dominant force in the formation of the various
states of western culture, including the contemporary state. And its ideas of God, humanity,
history, etc., have naturally been influential
in the development of our contemporary understanding of reality. Since our understanding
at any time influences the very character of our
experience in the future, a correlation between
Christian ideas and the modern experience of
reality should be expected. Indeed, it would be
surprising if there were not a strong correlation
at this point. Even ideas which prima facie
stand opposed to the Christian tradition, such
as modern secularism and atheism, can be shown
to have roots in the tradition. But just because the roots of these ideas are in the tradition, and there is consequently something of
a correlation between the Christian faith and
the modern understanding of reality, would not
in itself appear to indicate much about the
truth of the Christian faith, or of its epistemological superiority to other traditions.

      My criticism is again quite simple. It
seems to me that Pannenberg's ranking procedure
for religions is not able to distinguish between historical influence and truth. How would
we decide whether a strong correlation in this

case proves or even suggests that the Christian
God exists, and hence that Christian theology
should be ranked higher than that of other religions? For a Christian, perhaps, the correlation
would be further evidence of God's revelatory
power. But for a member of another religion or
a nonbeliever, the correlation might well indicate only historical influence.

In the third place, despite the considerable
amount of attention which Pannenberg devotes to
the subject, it is still by no means clear how
the program would be put into effect. The dirth
of examples which sometimes detracts from his
work is particularly hurtful in this case. He
writes at length on the correlation between
various Christian ideas and the modern understanding of reality; but this by itself does
not complete the procedure as he has described
it. Unfortunately, he provides very little in
the way of the comparative analysis which would
be required in order to rank religions, and
which is essential to the theological task as
he has outlined it. To be sure, this is a
difficult task, due to its novelty and boldness,
and perhaps it is asking too much to request
examples at this point. Such would certainly
help, however, in the effort to clarify just
how the procedure might work.

Pannenberg comes closest to such comparative analysis in the essay, "Toward a Theology
of the History of Religions," though even here
the analysis is carried out only on a very
general level. In this essay, he argues that
Christianity does not "finitize" the "divine
mystery" as other religions do, but records a
revelation in which the divine reality appears
"as infinite."[43] Ordinarily, he says, through
a "fixation onto a finite medium," religions
attempt to identify God with some particular object or place, thereby putting the infinite
being at their disposal, and closing their religion to the possibility of genuine temporal

transformation.[44] The divine appearance in Jesus,
in contrast, is infinite due to the fact that
the latter did not "bind God to his own person;"
rather, Jesus "sacrificed himself in obedience to
his mission."[45] He existed, in other words, not
for himself, but to point the way to the coming
of God's Kingdom. Because Jesus was willing to
sacrifice himself in this way to the will of God,
in this case the infinite being does not become
bound to the finite, but the finite is given over
to the infinite. Attention thus is directed away
from the medium to that which is revealed--God.[46]

Now, Pannenberg argues, the appearance of
the divine reality in history as infinite is
definitive in an important way for religious
consciousness. It is definitive "because it
would not displace but would instead disclose
the openness of the future, the noncloseability
of the history of mankind even with respect to
its knowledge of God."[47] In other words, Pannenberg is saying that the tendency of other religions to bind God to that which is finite can
be correlated with a closed and cyclical view
of history in which everything of essential importance is already known; but in the case of
Christianity there is a genuine openness to the
future because God appears in Christ precisely
as the infinite being. Since Christianity records the appearance of God in this way, the
door is opened for a continual development in
the knowledge of humankind. The essential
truths of history are not already known for the
infinite did not become bound to the finite man,
Jesus of Nazareth.

This argument is in a certain way attractive; it makes a nice theological point, especially for those in the liberal theological tradition. The revelation in Christ is the 'final'
revelation precisely because of its openness to
the future. Its very finality consists in its
openness. And further, this kind of assessment
demonstrates well the advancement of Christianity

67

beyond the conceptuality of primitive polytheistic and mythical religions. The monotheistic religions Judaism and Islam, however, are not so obviously upstaged by Christianity in the respect under consideration, and it is not clear to me how the testing procedure would work in these cases. Indeed, I suspect that their theologians would argue heatedly in regard to the issue of finitization. A longstanding aspect in the polemic of both Judaism and Islam against Christianity has been that the latter does in fact finitize the absolute by thinking of Jesus as God incarnate (whereas they refuse to identify anything finite with God). We might respond on behalf of Pannenberg that within certain sects of Judaism the infinite being is bound to a code of law and that within certain sects of Islam the infinite being is bound to a book. But these charges, of course, could also be made against certain sects of Christianity.

I frankly do not see how this conflict could be resolved and how one of the monotheistic religions could be ranked above the others in the respect mentioned. All three religions lay claim to a revelation of the divine as infinite. The only way in which a clear ranking could be established as to their respective determinative power over the modern idea of the openness of the future is to appeal again simply to historical influence itself, and not the conceptual priority which Pannenberg seems at least to want. In all likelihood, the Christian tradition has been more determinative purely as a historical influence. But as we noted above, this does not show the truth of Christianity.

Perhaps Pannenberg is not really concerned to rank Christianity above the other monotheistic religions. But if not, it is unclear just what significance the testing procedure has. As noted above, he thinks of God primarily in terms of the power to determine reality. Sometimes one receives the impression from his works that he has taken as his project the task of showing the omnipotence of the Christian God by demonstrating that Christian <u>ideas about</u> the omnipotence of God have been strongly influential in the development of western culture. Indeed, he is remarkably successful in the effort. But this, of course, is to conflate the power of an idea over other ideas and the power of a reality over other realities.

These reflections lead to a third and final point of criticism. We began this analysis by showing Pannenberg's desire to escape the subjective arbitrariness of much recent theology. In the effort to secure a more objective footing for theological claims, he accepted the notion that to be counted a science a field of inquiry must have some testing procedure which will be respected by those working in the field regardless of the presuppositions and biases which they may bring to the debate. And he spun out in that regard the procedure outlined above. Now, my basic question is the following: What is apt to be <u>settled</u> theologically by the use of the procedure?

A lot has been and will be accomplished by Christian theologians in respect to a demonstration of the illuminative significance of the Christian tradition for modern experience. But what is apt to be settled <u>comparatively</u>?

Pannenberg's conception of the scientific character of theology with its attendant objectivity leaves out, I suggest, a dimension of objectivity which is crucial for the question whether a field of inquiry constitutes a science. John Passmore, in his essay, "The Objectivity of History," argues like Pannenberg that the test of objectivity is not whether a claim corresponds to an actual state of affairs but whether there are "regular ways of settling issues, by the use of which men of whatever party can be brought to see what actually happened."[48]

69

Passmore argues, of course, that this criterion
is satisfied by many historical claims and not
by claims in the natural sciences alone. Pannenberg states a conception similar to Passmore's,
but does not emphasize the idea that some questions must get settled if we are indeed doing
science.

It is very difficult to see how the claim
of one tradition to superiority over the others
could be settled in a religiously-pluralistic
world, even in a tentative sense. No doubt,
scholars within the given traditions are able,
due to their hermeneutical skills, to show more
of the power of their own tradition than that
of rivals. But such a procedure is still bound
to subjectivity in a way in which the natural
sciences, to say the least, are not, and hence
could hardly be called 'scientific' or 'objective'.

I suggest, therefore, as a final point
of criticism, that if Pannenberg is saying that
theological claims of an intertraditional sort
can indeed be settled, even tentatively, he is
not providing an accurate assessment of the
pluralistic character of modern religious experience and theological commitments and the
strong attachment which theologians often quite
naturally exhibit to their own traditions. And
if he is not arguing that theological claims
of an intertraditional sort can be settled,
there is a serious omission in the conception
of the objectivity which a field of inquiry
must have in order to be counted a science.

By way of summary, then, I argue that the
comparative aspect of Pannenberg's work on a
testing procedure for theological claims is
flawed in three respects. First, it requires
a uniformity in the modern experience of reality
which is simply absent. Second, it shows only
that some ideas are historically more influential
than others, not that they are true. And third,

it cannot rank the monotheistic conceptions of God in terms of comprehensive and integrative power. I suggest, then, that the procedure lacks the power to settle issues in the really crucial sense, and thus to establish theology as a science.

These criticisms do not undermine what really is, I think, the more important aspect of the procedure--the illuminative hermeneutical project described above. The next chapters will contain an assessment of Pannenberg's most significant contributions in this regard. My point here is only that it is a misnomer to think of theology as a science if by that one were to suppose that issues of an intertraditional sort can be settled therein as issues are settled in the natural and social sciences.

NOTES

[1]This essay is the revised form of a lecture delivered in 1962, and it is included in BQT, 2:65-118.

[2]"Toward a Theology," p. 67.

[3]Ibid., pp. 67-71.   [4]Ibid., pp. 70, 112.

[5]Ibid., p. 70.

[6]TPS, pp. 320-21. Actually, Pannenberg distinguishes here, after Hans Reichenbach, the "heuristic" and "probative" contexts of theological statements. I take his intention to be the same as that standing behind the widely-accepted analytic distinction between discovery and justification. The following explanatory comment, for instance, could fit either distinction: "Confusion between the two is most likely where a personal religious conviction is used as the basis for an argument for which intersubjective validity is sumultaneously claimed" (TPS, p. 321).

[7]"Toward a Theology," p. 71.

[8]Ibid., pp. 70-80.   [9]Ibid., p. 80.

[10]Ibid., p. 97.   [11]Ibid., p. 112.

[12]TPS, pp. 297-345.   [13]Ibid., p. 299.

[14]Ibid., p. 301.

[15]For the publication details, see n. 4, p. 46.

[16]TPS, pp. 302-3.   [17]Ibid., p. 303.

[18]TPS, p. 310. My translation is based on the German in Wissenschaftstheorie, p. 312.

[19] TPS, pp. 310-14.   [20] Ibid., p. 310.

[21] Ibid., p. 314.   [22] Ibid., p. 316.

[23] Ibid., p. 168.   [24] Ibid.

[25] Ibid., p. 329.   [26] Ibid., pp. 329-30.

[27] Ibid., p. 330.   [28] Ibid., pp. 50-58.

[29] Ibid., pp. 320-21.

[30] "Toward a Theology," p. 82.

[31] TPS, p. 316. My translation is based on the German in Wissenschaftstheorie, pp. 318-19.

[32] Human Nature, Election, and History (Philadelphia: Westminster Press, 1977), p. 14.

[33] "The Nature of a Theological Statement," Zygon 7 (March 1972):12.

[34] TPS, p. 315.   [35] Ibid.

[36] Ibid., p. 309.   [37] Ibid., pp. 337-38.

[38] Ibid., pp. 339-41.   [39] Ibid., p. 340.

[40] This conception of the modern understanding of reality is expressed by Pannenberg in a variety of places, most forcibly in his little anthropological work, What is Man?, trans. Duane A. Priebe (Philadelphia: Fortress Press, 1970), and in his essay, "What is Truth?" in BQT, 2:1-27. I shall develop the concept of Weltoffenheit in greater detail in chapters four and five, where it plays a large role in the discussions of the Resurrection and of the relation between divine power and human freedom.

[41] TPS, p. 332.   [42] Ibid., pp. 339-45.

[43] "Toward a Theology," pp. 105-10.

[44]Ibid., pp. 108-9.   [45]Ibid., p. 114.

[46]Ibid.   [47]Ibid., p. 110.

[48]John A. Passmore, "The Objectivity of History," in Philosophical Analysis and History, ed. William H. Dray (New York: Harper and Row, 1966), p. 91.

Chapter Four

THE RESURRECTION ARGUMENT

Pannenberg is probably better known for
his defense of the historical factuality of
Jesus' Resurrection than for any other aspect
of his thought. Indeed, when his Resurrection
argument first became known in the United States
in the mid-sixties, it appeared for a time that
conservative theologians in general would make
of Pannenberg a new champion. When the details
of his argument were closely examined, the in-
fatuation of conservative scholarship diminished
somewhat; but the impression that Pannenberg's
treatment of the Resurrection represents a bold
and creative move in theology has lingered in
all theological camps. In my opinion, no one
has yet responded to his argument in a comprehensive and persuasive fashion.[1] In fact, to
my knowledge, no one at all has responded from
the standpoint of philosophy of religion. This
is a marvel because it is really addressed primarily to philosophers, not historians or theologians.

Before taking up the argument itself, we
should note that Pannenberg's interest in defen-
ding the factuality of the Resurrection represents
a significant departure from the dominant tendency of modern Protestant thought. As is well-
known, neither Barth nor Bultmann considered the
factuality of the Resurrection a legitimate question for historical scholarship. In this regard,
Barth put forward the baffling notion that the
Resurrection was a historical event which is not
open to critical inquiry;[2] and Bultmann advanced
the more radical view that the Resurrection is
not open to historical inquiry precisely because
it is not a historical event.[3] These respective
positions reflect the fundamental tendency of
dialectical theology to play down the historical

Jesus in favor of the Christ of faith. Since
this approach to theology is philosophically
grounded in Kantian dualism, the realm of fact,
or the phenomenal world, is thought to be of
little consequence so far as a basis for faith
is concerned. Christologically, this means
that the primary interest of theology should
not be Historie, the actual events in Jesus'
life, but Geschichte, the significance of the
Christ-idea for believers.[4]

Pannenberg is among the handful of contemporary theologians who have reacted against
this preoccupation with Geschichte by initiating
a new quest for the historical Jesus. He rejects
the dualism of Historie and Geschichte, and holds
that the kerygma must either be based on actual
historical events or be given up as fantasy. In
an early essay, "The Doctrine of Revelation," he
makes his position very clear: "The historical
revelation is open to anyone who has eyes to
see."[5] (Contrast, for instance, the Bultmannian
claim that revelation is visible only to the
"eyes of faith.") In Pannenberg's view, then,
revelation cannot be separated from historical
facts. Moreover, the facts which undergird faith
are not, in his opinion, somehow inaccessible to
historical inquiry. If we assert that the Resurrection took place at a particular time and place
in history, then we are claiming that it was a
historical event. And in that case we must allow,
argues Pannenberg, that it is accessible to critical research just like other historical events.

If the Resurrection is open to critical
research, and if the fundamental task of the
systematic theologian is, as Pannenberg believes,
to argue on all fronts in support of his tradition, it becomes important to work out a defense
for the historical factuality of the Resurrection.
Such a defense should not rest on faith-assump-
tions at any point, including the question of the
reliability of biblical texts. Thus, Pannenberg
seeks to defend the Resurrection in the light of

the very best of modern critical scholarship.

The Meaning of 'Resurrection'

He begins by attempting to clarify the
meaning of the expression 'resurrection of the
dead'. In a difficult but important statement,
Pannenberg says,

> To speak about the resurrection of the dead
> is not comparable to speaking about any ran-
> dom circumstance which can be identified
> empirically at any time. Here we are
> dealing, rather, with a metaphor.[6]

This statement contains two ideas which are fundamental to his position. In the first place,
the resurrection of the dead is obviously not
a part of our ordinary experience. Indeed, no
one actually observed the Resurrection of Christ.
We have no way of knowing what, if anything, an
actual witness to his Resurrection would have
seen. Our only testimony in connection with
the event comes from those who claim to have
encountered Christ after the Resurrection.
Hence, when we speak of a resurrection of the
dead, we do not know from empirical experience
(or from any other source, for that matter)
exactly what kind of process we are talking
about.

In the second place, it follows from the
fact that we have no empirical experience of a
resurrection that our speech regarding such must
be metaphorical in character. The specific metaphor which is consistently employed in Scripture
in this regard is 'rising from sleep'. Pannenberg calls attention to the fact that throughout the Bible death is thought of as sleep, and
correspondingly the Resurrection is pictured as
awakening and rising from sleep.[7] It is important

77

to note this metaphorical character of biblical expressions regarding the Resurrection, for it will prevent us from supposing that we have a precise and understandable concept of the reality of the event. As Pannenberg puts it,

> The intended reality is beyond the experience of the man who lives on this side of death. Thus the only possible mode of speaking about it is metaphorical, using images of this-worldly occurrences.[8]

This metaphorical structure of speech about the Resurrection, however, does not in any way entail that it is somehow removed from the realm of historical reality investigated by the historian. Whether or not the Resurrection happened is a matter of debate. The precise nature of the process involved in the Resurrection and indeed the very nature of the Resurrected Christ himself elude our understanding.

In addition to these preliminary comments regarding the nature of the Resurrection and of speech about it, Pannenberg identifies two common misconceptions which he is at pains to avoid. On the one hand, he carefully guards against confusing resurrection with the resuscitation of a physical body. And on the other hand, he distinguishes resurrection and immortality.

Concerning the distinction between resurrection and resuscitation, Pannenberg believes it to be quite significant that the earliest recorded Christian conception of resurrection (contained in the first letter of Paul to the Church at Corinth) does not view it as the resuscitation of a body. A revived body, he points out, would not be fundamentally different from the living bodies which we encounter in ordinary experience. But the reality which confronted the disciples as the risen Christ was experienced as something fundamentally new. Paul speaks of this reality as an imperishable "spiritual body."[9] The importance of this understanding is found in the fact that it removes the Resurrection of Christ from the category of the bodily resuscitations which are reported in ancient literature (including the resuscitations accomplished by Jesus himself).[10] Pannenberg is inclined to view these miracle stories, even those in the gospels, as legendary. But more importantly, the individuals who were supposedly brought back to life by the miracle-workers of the ancient world were not basically changed in the process of being revived. These individuals would die again. Resurrection is different, Pannenberg says, in that the individual who is raised from the dead undergoes a fundamental "transformation" (Verwandlung).[11] In contrast to the resuscitated body of Lazarus, for instance, the resurrected body of Jesus was imperishable. He would not die again.

Concerning the distinction between resurrection and immortality, Pannenberg picks up on a theme which has long been characteristic of Protestant scholarship. Protestant theologians have generally made use of this distinction in their efforts to separate biblical and Hebrew conceptions from Greek ideas which were superimposed upon them in the early centuries of Christian history. Immortality, according to the customary Protestant view, was a distinctively Greek idea. The Hebrews did not accept the notion that the human being is a composite of body and soul or the belief that some particular part of a human being will not die.

Pannenberg is especially concerned to correlate the Hebrew belief regarding an afterlife with their eschatological expectations. In this context, he points out, the idea of an immortal soul is simply out of place. The Hebrews expected something new and different with the coming of the Kingdom. The idea of immortality, however, is not focused on the novel and futural but on the preservation of an indestructible "kernel" of our present existence.12 As the Hebrews understood it, then, and as Pannenberg himself understands it, resurrection should not be confused with the continued existence after death of an immortal soul. It is rather the coming alive again of a person who was wholly dead.

In summary of this first section, Pannenberg holds that the Resurrection is a historical event, though the nature of the resurrected Jesus and the process of resurrection elude our understanding. What happened to Jesus is best expressed with the metaphor 'rising from sleep'. And we can conceptualize the relation between the pre- and post-Easter Jesus in terms of the transformation of his body. The resurrected Jesus, according to this picture, has a spiritual body which is no longer subject to death. This body is not just the revived original; and its spiritual nature should not be conceived as the continued existence of a soul.

Now to the argument itself. Some of Pannenberg's claims about the Resurrection are basically historical in character and others are basically philosophical. Hence I shall speak of the historical and philosophical 'phases' of the argument. It seems to me that the historical material is primarily important not because of its persuasiveness as a historical account but because it further clarifies how Pannenberg wants to think of the Resurrection. This being the case, I shall simply state the historical phase without the detailed analysis which a historian would provide for it. After touching base with the historical phase in this way, I shall take up the philosophical claims in considerable detail; for this is where the real thrust of the argument can be felt.

Historical Considerations

There are basically two groups of stories in the Resurrection tradition in the New Testament. One group speaks of the Resurrection through an account of the appearances of the resurrected Lord. The other group speaks of the event through the story of the empty tomb. I shall call these after Pannenberg the 'appearance tradition' and the 'empty tomb tradition'.

Pannenberg gives primary attention to the appearance tradition and especially to the Pauline understanding of it. Sometimes it is overlooked that Paul himself claims to have encountered the risen Lord. At the conclusion of a list of eyewitnesses, he says that Christ appeared to him "last of all" (I Cor. 15:8). Paul wrote the letter in which this list occurs in approximately A.D. 56. This makes his list of witnesses, including himself, the earliest documentation of the appearances (if the traditional date for Mark, A.D. 64, is accepted).

Not only is Paul's the earliest record, but it is also, according to Pannenberg, the only record we have from anyone who claims to have seen the resurrected Christ.[13] If this is true, then Paul's account of his experience and his understanding of the Resurrection are matters of the utmost theological importance.

Paul's account of the experience is recorded in three different places in the book of Acts (9:1-9; 22:6-12; and 26:12-18). According to biblical scholars, Acts should be dated at the earliest during the seventh decade A.D. and perhaps as late as the ninth decade A.D.[14] If the former dating is accepted, approximately ten years lapsed between the time when Paul first mentioned his encounter in the letter to the Corinthians and the time when it was recorded in Acts, and if the latter dating is accepted, as many as thirty years lapsed. The account in Acts

refers to an experience which Paul had a few
years after Christ was cricified (not within the
forty-day limit set by the traditional understanding of the Resurrection and Ascension)
while traveling to Damascus with some friends
for the purpose of bringing to a halt the spread
of Christianity there. According to these accounts, Paul saw a light of such brilliance that
it temporarily blinded him and he heard the voice
of Christ.

Pannenberg allows that it is impossible to
say exactly what Paul experienced on the road to
Damascus. He maintains, however, that at least
the following statements are probably true: Paul
experienced an appearance "from heaven" so to
speak (unlike the accounts in the gospels where
Jesus meets with the disciples, walks about with
them, etc.); and what Paul saw was not an earthly,
resuscitated corpse. Whatever he experienced,
it is certain that he identified the object of
the experience with Jesus and understood the
appearance as confirmation of the central message of Christianity--that Christ was risen from
the dead.[15]

Paul's experience, of course, was not the
only purported encounter with the risen Christ.
The gospels recount a number of appearances.
Though the details of these stories may be
questionable, Pannenberg thinks that it is
important to note that the appearance stories
were in circulation rather soon after Jesus was
crucified and that Paul links his own experience
with these other encounters, apparently thinking
of it as essentially the same kind of experience
as the disciples had.[16]

Of course, the appearance tradition does
not prove without further argument that Jesus
was really raised from the dead. It is possible
that the experiences of the disciples were purely subjective in nature, that they were psychologically induced through rising expectations

grounded ultimately in the tales of a few early encounters, etc. Pannenberg argues against such a position, saying that the "subjective vision" hypothesis is insufficient to account for the material under consideration for two reasons.

In the first place, there was a plurality of appearances and they were distributed over a period of several years. It may be that such a chain of visions could be induced through the turmoil of early Christian frustration and the excitement created by one or two stories, but the complexity of the appearance tradition weighs against this hypothesis.[17]

In the second place, the subjective vision hypothesis fails to account for the enthusiasm and dedication of the early Christians. The followers of Christ were confused and defeated at the time of the Crucifixion. Although according to scripture Jesus had attempted to prepare them for both his death and Resurrection, they did not really seem to expect the Resurrection. Pannenberg points out in this connection that if the disciples accepted the prevailing tradition of the period, they expected only a general resurrection at the end of time. They had little basis for the expectation that one individual would be raised before all the others and before the end of history. In the light of their general disappointment over the death of Jesus, and the absence of any strong expectation that he would be raised from the dead prior to the end of time, Pannenberg argues that an actual Resurrection and appearance of Christ is the best hypothesis to account for the fact that the disciples could suddenly have renewed fervor.[18]

The empty tomb tradition further enforces the claim that Christ was raised from the dead. From a purely historical standpoint, Pannenberg reasons, the claim that the tomb was empty is probably true. This claim was made in Jerusalem.

It could have been refuted simply by showing that the dead body was still in the tomb. But there is nothing either in the gospels or in the early polemic against the Christian message which would indicate any doubt that the tomb was in fact empty.[19]

One additional historical consideration enters into Pannenberg's argument. It appears that the two traditions were transmitted independently of one another in the early years of Christianity. The disciples apparently went back to Galilee upon the death of Jesus, and the appearances, by and large, took place there. The empty tomb occurred, of course, in Jerusalem. Pannenberg maintains that the independence of the two traditions adds weight to the Christian claim.[20]

From the probability that the appearance tradition (with the Pauline accent) is reliable, that the tomb was indeed empty, and that the two traditions circulated independently, Pannenberg concludes that it is likely that Jesus was raised from the dead. He is aware, however, that modern disbelief in the Resurrection has more to do with certain philosophical commitments than a dirth of historical proof. Hence, in addition to these historical considerations, he puts forward several philosophical claims which are intended to clear the way for acceptance of the argument as a whole. I shall take up the most important of these claims.

Philosophical Considerations

The first philosophical claim is the assertion that the Resurrection is not scientifically impossible. By this claim, Pannenberg intends to repudiate an apriori prescriptivism which would deny the possibility of the Resurrection from the very beginning. In support of his

contention, he argues essentially that the modern
understanding of natural laws precludes definitive
judgments as to the possibility of an event's oc-
currence. He shows first why this is the case
regarding future events, and then applies the
same line of reasoning to past events.

Regarding the future, Pannenberg calls
attention to the fact that it is not possible to
predict with certainty what will or will not happen. There are basically two reasons for this:
(1) The 'laws' of nature themselves can be accepted as scientific statements only because
they allow for the possibility of falsification.
They cannot be considered absolutely certain in
the sense that further experience is irrelevant
to the question of their truth. Pannenberg expresses this point by saying that the natural
laws are contingent. They depend on the dis-
coveries and testing procedures of the scientific
community which is itself constantly altering its
understanding of reality in the process of its
historical development.[21] (2) The natural laws
currently available do not exhaust every aspect
of any event. There is always something more
to be explained in any event than can be explained by presently-known laws due to the fact
that each event is in some respect novel. Pannenberg expresses this incompleteness of the set
of natural laws by saying that they are abstractions from the fullness of an event.[22]

No one will dispute his claim that the
future cannot be predicted with certainty upon
the basis of natural laws. Obviously, we are
not in position to say that such and such an
event cannot occur in the future (so long as it
is not described in contradictory terms). Pannenberg says that this same principle must hold
also in regard to the past. As we cannot predict with certainty, neither can we retrodict
with certainty. We are not in position to say
that such and such an event could not have occurred in the past (again, so long as it is not

85

described in contradictory terms). If natural laws were absolute, and if we had a complete set of such, then we could prescribe in an apriori way what can and cannot happen. Unfortunately, or in the case of the theologian, fortunately, that is not the case.[23]

From the fact that we cannot, generally speaking, prescribe from the outset what can and cannot happen, Pannenberg infers that the Resurrection cannot be ruled out on the basis of natural laws. He is not content, however, merely to secure the theoretical possibility of the event. He also attempts to secure for it a measure of scientific respectability by arguing that the Resurrection is not necessarily out of accord with known laws of science. In this connection, he makes use of the distinction noted above between transformation and resuscitation. If resurrection is interpreted in terms of resuscitation, Pannenberg says, we would have to conclude that the Resurrection of Christ would "hardly be thinkable."[24] The reason for this conclusion is obvious. We are well-acquainted with the "irreversible processes of dissolution" which set in after death. Though resuscitation cannot be ruled out altogether on a theoretical basis, it would have to be excluded as a practical possibility. In contrast, the process of transformation is not unthinkable, becuase in this case we know only the "starting point," but not the "final point" of the process.[25]

In other words, we know enough from biology and chemistry about the decomposition-process to judge a resuscitation highly unlikely. Such would be, we might say, out of keeping with the laws of nature which are presently available. In contrast, we know nothing about a process of divine transformation. Hence, it is not necessarily out of keeping with the laws of nature which we presently have. Rather, a transformation transcends these laws. We do not have the requisite knowledge for understanding such a process now, though we may at some later date.

The most obvious criticism of Pannenberg's argument from a scientific standpoint would focus on the conception of the event as a divine act. How, it might be asked, can the Resurrection be made compatible with natural science if it is thought of as a divine act? Ordinarily, the argument might continue, such a conception would imply that God somehow interrupts the course of nature. But if this is so, then how is it possible that a scientific explanation might be given for the event in question? Such an explanation would seem to be out of place, because the event depends ultimately on God, not any of the natural causes investigated by scientists.

Pannenberg's account circumvents this criticism nicely, due to his conception of divine action. As we shall see in chapter five, in his view every event is in a certain sense a divine act, and hence it is not really even possible to distinguish (in his account) natural events and divine acts. Pannenberg elucidates this notion with the suggestion that God acts precisely through natural laws, that is, in such a way that no interruption of the natural course is required. "God has limited himself in his contingent acts by definite laws, and he works in their framework."[26] This does not mean, of course, that divine action merely consists in a monotonous repetition of predictable events. Quite the contrary, Pannenberg holds that in the course of nature and in accord with natural laws, God is constantly introducing novelty into the universe through the uniqueness and unrepeatability of each historical event. Presumably, then, in the case of the Resurrection, God acted in accord with natural laws (albeit again laws which we do not presently have) to introduce the most profound novelty of all history.

As on other issues, Pannenberg is suggesting

at this point that traditional incompatibilities
may be overcome. Here he seeks to work around
the supposed incompatibility of natural science
and the Resurrection by dealing critically both
with the Christian tradition and the commitments
of modernity. In regard to the tradition, he
asks that the longstanding distinction between
divine, supernatural or miraculous, acts and
natural events be reworked. He, of course, is
not the first to make such a suggestion. But
his project assumes peculiar importance since
it is worked out with full awareness of the
developments in science and the philosophy of
science in the twentieth century. If the Resurrection can be conceived as an act of God in
accord with natural laws, though laws presently
unknown, then from the theological side the incompatibility between the Resurrection and natural science is removed. From the side of
contemporary science, however, there may remain
a problem. If presently-accepted laws are absolutized, and if one holds, as many seem to,
that nothing can happen which cannot be described
by those laws, then an incompatibility remains.
Hence, Pannenberg asks for a critical approach
even to the revered natural laws of modern
science. If one can avoid absolutizing them,
then from the side of science the incompatibility
between the Resurrection and natural science is
also removed.

Though I shall question later the notion
that every event must be seen as a divine act,
it seems to me that Pannenberg's first philosophical claim--that the Resurrection is not
incompatible with science--is successful, given
the reconstructions which he suggest.

Pannenberg seeks, of course, not only to
relate the Resurrection to the work of the
natural scientist but also, and more directly,
to the work of the historian. His second basic
philosophical claim, then, is that the Resurrection should not be excluded from the domain

of events investigated by historians. At first
glance, this seems to be a mere repetition of the
theological point with which this chapter began,
namely, Pannenberg's insistence that the Resurrection is not a privileged event which is somehow immune to historical criticism. Upon deeper
inspection, however, these two claims are significantly different. The earlier claim was
addressed to theologians and was theologically
motivated. The claim under consideration here
is addressed to historians and is philosophically
motivated. In this case, Pannenberg is not wor-
ried about the theologian's tendency to remove
the Resurrection from the stream of historical
events. Rather, he is concerned about the historian's tendency simply to ignore the Resurrection.

       By and large, secular historians do ignore
it. Why is this? Pannenberg believes that they
shy away on the basis of a particular methodological commitment. Historians are generally
committed, he says, to a "principle of analogy"
(not to be confused with the analogia entis)
in their investigation of past events. This
principle, as he describes it, says that "something difficult to understand, comparatively
opaque, should be conceived and assessed from
the standpoint of that which is familiar to the
investigator."[27] The general value of such a
principle is incontestable. Pannenberg contends,
however, that it is easily turned into a con-
striction of open-minded inquiry. This occurs,
he says, when one postulates a "fundamental
homogeneity (Gleichartigkeit) of all reality
with the current range of experience and research."[28]

       In less opaque language, Pannenberg is
objecting to the idea that every event of all
times and places must be seen as just another
instance of some type of event with which we
are already familiar. Through such a procedure,
a genuinely-unique event, one which "bursts

analogies" with more normal events, would simply be overlooked.[29] Pannenberg's challenge to the historian here is similar to his challenge to the natural scientist above. As the scientist cannot eliminate the possibility of the Resurrection on the basis of natural law, so the historian cannot discount reports of events solely because the events described therein are significantly different from the ordinary.

The principle of analogy, Pannenberg contends, is a useful tool only so long as it allows one to see that which is similar in non-homogeneous events, that is, so long as it allows one to respect the individual peculiarity of each event. Given the widely-accepted view that the historian studies the particular rather than the general, his or her task demands that the principle of analogy not be allowed to cover up the uniqueness of events. This is an especially-important concern for Pannenberg, because he maintains that the revelation of God is particularly apparent precisely in events which are startling due to their unlikely, or extraordinary character.[30] To decide beforehand that the individual peculiarities of events will be ignored or levelled down in terms of analogy is to proscribe beforehand the possibility of revelation as he understands it.

The relevance of this concern to the Resurrection is obvious. If the event purported to be a Resurrection by Christians is taken on the analogy of other events more accessible to the modern scholar, then the Resurrection cannot be accepted as a historical fact regardless of the evidence put forward on its behalf. Pannenberg states his case in this regard very forcibly:

> Does not the postulate of the fundamental homogeneity of all events usually form the chief argument against the historicity of the Resurrection of Jesus? But if that is so, does not the opinion, which has come to

be regarded as virtually self-evident, that the Resurrection of Jesus cannot be a historical event, rest on a remarkably weak foundation? Only the particular characteristics of the reports about it make it possible to judge the historicity of the Resurrection, not the prejudgment that every event must be fundamentally of the same kind as every other.[31]

On the surface, these comments seem to be innocent enough. It appears that Pannenberg has a legitimate complaint. He is simply asking historians to be fair. In reality, however, the position involves a very significant difficulty for historiography. Pannenberg seems to be asking the historian, even the secular historian, to consider the Resurrection as an act of God as a possible explanation for the emergence of primitive Christianity. The immediate and obvious question is whether appeal to divine agency is not off-limits to the historian qua historian.

This objection is stated very clearly in a critique of Pannenberg's argument by Herbert Burhenn. Burhenn points out that a historian is not free to roam at will in regard to explanations. As he understands it, the historian's explanations depend on a "body of common-sense knowledge" which is shared by most educated persons. Included in such a body of knowledge would be basic information concerning the physical world, human behavior, social institutions, etc.[32] Burhenn is not speaking of a technical knowledge of these areas, such as would be possessed by the requisite specialists, but the everyday knowledge of the educated person. He admits that the boundaries of this body of knowledge are imprecise, and that within it certain beliefs are more widely held than others.[33] Despite the lack of precision, however, Burhenn feels that there clearly exists such a body of common-sense knowledge to which the historian can appeal without having to defend his appeal.

I am inclined to agree with Burhenn. This sort of claim is vary familiar in the philosophy of history. Quite frequently, those philosophers who oppose the Hempelian Covering Law Model will cite just such an everyday kind of knowledge as the general resource material for historical explanation. Michael Scriven, for instance, speaks in this regard of "normic" generalizations, or our everyday knowledge of what happens in normal situations.[34] The historian depends, he says, upon a "general knowledge of human nature" in contrast to a specialized "scientific knowledge."[35]

Burhenn next applies his notion of a body of common-sense knowledge to Pannenberg's argument. He maintains that there are probably no "specifically religious principles" in this body of knowledge at the present time (though he allows that there may be a few ethical principles).[36] This contention, of course, depends on his subjective reading of the degree of secularization in modern culture. Again, I am inclined to agree with his assessment.[37]

Now, upon certain occasions, says Burhenn, it may be necessary for a historian to go beyond the body of common-sense knowledge. He may appeal, for instance, to a law of physics or a statistical study in the social sciences, matters which are understood only by the specialists in these fields. Since he is not writing for a readership which has technical knowledge in the relevant fields, however, his appeal must be defended in some way. He should offer at least a brief explanation of the concepts involved and a brief justification for their use in the particular situation under consideration. Especially if the material to which he appeals is of doubtful validity, he should say why he uses that specific material rather than alternatives.[38]

The direction of Burhenn's argument is now

clear. Pannenberg wants historians to consider seriously the traditional Christian explanation for the emergence of primitive Christianity. But this explanation depends on the notion of an act of God, a specialized concept. Such a concept is not part of the body of common-sense knowledge to which a historian ordinarily appeals. Therefore, to use it a historian would need to defend the concept, presumably through an argument for the truth of theism. But at this point, the original explanation is bound to get hopelessly bogged down. For a long time, there has been no general agreement on the truth of theism, and no such agreement seems to be looming on the horizon. In the absence of this general agreement, however, an appeal to divine agency would appear to be off-limits to the historian as a historian.

In order to prevent misunderstanding, several qualifications of this criticism should be stated. First, my criticism of Pannenberg in this regard does not mean that the Resurrection is incompatible with critical historiography. It means only that a historian, because of his or her methodology, is not in position to use the Resurrection as an explanation for the emergence of early Christianity due to the fact that such would depend on the specialized concept of divine agency. The impossibility of using the Resurrection as an explanation is not, of course, the same thing as the impossibility of allowing that the Resurrection occurred. From the standpoint of the critical, secular historian, the Resurrection may or may not have happened. I am saying only that the historian is not at liberty, at least in present circumstances, to use it in the writing of history.

Second, my criticism does not mean that a historian cannot or should not investigate the facts surrounding the purported Resurrection. The historian strives for objectivity, and should look at the evidence for what it is worth. But

93

Pannenberg seems to think not only that the historian must give serious consideration to the Resurrection, but also that he or she must come to a decision concerning the likelihood of its havine occurred. But this seems plainly false. As Burhenn points out, the historian as a historian is not faced with decisions of "great existential import."[39] In cases where the evidence is insufficient to warrant a decision for one side or the other, the historian may exercise the prerogative simply to defer judgment.[40] Especially in a case in which the evidence points toward the strange conclusion that a man rose from the dead, the most responsible attitude of a historian would appear to be non-commitment.[41] Even if the historical argument for the Resurrection is strong, then, the historian is not under a methodological obligation to endorse it as fact in the writing of history. It is altogether possible, and even intellectually responsible, to view the events surrounding the Resurrection as mysterious without coming to a definitive stance regarding the historical factuality of the Resurrection itself.

Third, my criticism does not mean that the Resurrection is not a good explanation for the emergence of primitive Christianity. I say only that at the present time it cannot be included in the writing of history as a good historical explanation. The historian is bound by the common-sense beliefs of his milieu. Times may change. People may again accept the existence of God as part of their body of assumptions about the world. At that time, the historian could offer the Resurrection as a viable explanation.

Fourth, and finally, my criticism does not mean that it is impossible for a contemporary historian to use the Resurrection as an explanation. It only throws considerable doubt upon the possibilities for success in such an undertaking. The historian who would appeal to the

Resurrection takes it upon himself or herself
to supply a defense of theism, a task of no
small proportions (but one from which Pannenberg,
I have to confess, does not shy away). And the
situation is especially perplexing if the historian is attempting to use the Resurrection as
a basic argument for the truth of theism.

Pannenberg's second philosophical claim,
therefore, I think to be less than successful.
He calls attention in a very insightful way to
the prejudices of contemporary historiography
and perhaps modernity itself, but, so far as I
can see, he is unable to show that the secular
historian should take up the details of the
Resurrection and incorporate such in historical
explanations.

The third, and last, part of the philosophical phase which warrants extensive treatment is Pannenberg's insistence that the idea
of a destiny beyond the grave is implicit in
modern philosophical assumptions about human
existence.[42] He thinks that it is extremely
important to establish the truth of this claim.
The Resurrection, he points out, was believable
to first-century Hebrews because they already
expected a general resurrection. In other words,
they had the requisite presuppositions for belief
in the Resurrection of Jesus. Pannenberg holds
that unless we can somehow share these presuppositions, it will be impossible for us to accept the Resurrection.[43] Of course, we cannot
simply adopt the apocalyptic expectations of
first-century Hebrews, as though nineteen centuries of philosophical development did not
exist. We can, however, ask whether there is
anything in the modern experience of reality
which might allow us at least to make contact
with the apocalyptic expectations regarding a
general resurrection.

Pannenberg finds this point of contact in
the idea of Weltoffenheit, openness to the world,

or perhaps better, the future, a concept which
was first mentioned in the third chapter and
which will play a large role in the discussion
of God and freedom in the next chapter. Though
a detailed treatment of the concept will be
reserved for chapter five, we recall from the
discussion above that it involves basically
the human capacity to transcend the present
in the light of possibilities for the future.
Pannenberg argues that this openness to the
world has rather obvious implications for the
question of human destiny. It means, he says,
that human beings are never finally satisfied
in any particular finite, or this-worldly,
condition. As a being open to the world, one
cannot accept the identification of his or her
ultimate destiny with such a condition. The
concept of openness implies that we must always
press on in our pursuit of fulfillment, even
beyond death. It implies an openness "that goes
beyond every finite situation."[44] Such an openness beyond the finite is tantamount, Pannenberg
contends, to the identification of one's destiny
with some condition beyond the grave.

He expands somewhat on this argument by
attending to what might be called the "phenomenology of hope." Pannenberg points out that the
motivation for the unending human search is the
hope for a better situation than we presently
have. But if human hope for the future runs
up against death as an absolute limit, then Sartre
is right: The human project in general is absurd.
In a vein similar to Kant's proof for immortality,
Pannenberg contends, "If death is the end, then
all hope for a coming fulfillment of existence
seems to be foolish."[45] Since in this case, hope
becomes impossible, the motivation for the human
pursuit of better conditions is lost, and presumably along with it the continual openness that
characterizes human existence. Openness to the
world and hope for the future, then, actually
imply openness to and hope for a future beyond
the world.

In response to this argument, it should be noted to begin with that it is very difficult to tell whether Pannenberg is providing a description of human existence or a prescription for it when he speaks of <u>Weltoffenheit</u>. He speaks of the never-ending search for fulfillment, a search which must be pushed on, he says, into the afterlife, as though it were a fact about human existence. Yet many individuals in the modern world do not in fact locate their destiny beyond the grave. If Pannenberg's comments are supposed to be descriptive, then either they are incorrect or a lot of modern individuals are not fully human. In point of fact, I doubt that the comments are meant to be descriptive. It seems, rather, that he has offered a prescription, saying in effect that if we accept certain generally-existentialistic beleifs about existence, and if we are willing to pursue with rigor their logical implications, we shall be forced to accept the belief that there will be an afterlife. We ought to believe in the afterlife, in other words, though in fact many moderns do not.

The most obvious doubt which one might entertain about this argument arises from a general survey of the existentialist approach to which Pannenberg is appealing. Such a survey reveals that there is certainly no consensus to the effect that one's ultimate destiny must be located beyond the grave. Indeed, the most influential existentialists--Heidegger and Sartre--assume a very negative stance toward an afterlife. Sartre, for instance, would place belief in an existence which continues beyond death together with all other religious securities in the category of 'bad faith'. And Heidegger insists that an authentic existence is predicated on the possibility that one view death as something which cannot be circumvented in any way.

Just because Sartre and Heidegger oppose the idea of an afterlife, however, does not mean that

97

it is impossible to support such an idea within the general framework of existentialism. The work of Kierkegaard would without doubt attest to the possibility of an existentialist accommodation of the afterlife. Pannenberg seems to be picking up on Kierkegaard's insight that when our moral existence breaks down, there is still the higher, religious existence, an existence which is oriented finally to the eternal rather than the temporal. What Pannenberg wants to say in this regard is that existentialists such as Sartre and Heidegger who deny an afterlife are fostering ultimately a kind of existence which is diametrically opposed to the openness to which they give lip-service. If one views death as the end of all hope, then there is no real openness to the future for this life with its present dimensions has been absolutized.

Though this argument is in ways appealing, on a logical basis it does not finally compel assent. The central claim is that if openness to the world means that one must locate his or her destiny beyond every finite situation, then it also means that one must locate his or her destiny beyond the grave. This claim is, I believe, an example of the fallacy in reasoning sometimes called 'composition'. Pannenberg argues that a property of the members of a collection must also be a property of the collection itself. Just because we must locate our destiny beyond each finite condition is not in itself a basis for the claim that we must locate our destiny beyond the totality of finite conditions. Again, regarding hope a similar mistake is made. Here Pannenberg argues that if death is the ultimate end of human existence, then hope is foolish if not impossible. This assertion, unfortunately, overlooks the possibility that hope need not be absolute. We can ordinarily hope for a better situation than any particular situation in which we find ourselves, and this improved situation need not be a state of perfect happiness. Granted, it may be very difficult in certain excruciating situations to have hope for the future apart from belief in an afterlife.[46] This in itself, however, does not show that hope is foolish or impossible in general apart from such a belief. There are many possible objects of human hope. An afterlife is one, a very important one indeed; but there are others.

In summary, then, Pannenberg's third philosophical claim is interesting but not logically compelling. He has shown that belief in the Resurrection is <u>not incompatible</u> with the implications of modern philosophical commitments of a basically-existentialistic sort, but he has not shown that those commitments <u>require</u> a belief in the afterlife.

General Assessment of the Argument

If the philosophical phase had been totally successful, Pannenberg would have shown that the Resurrection is not incompatible with modern science, that it ought to be used by historians if after thorough investigation they believe that it is the best explanation for the emergence of primitive Christianity, and that the modern world-view, or at least a dominant modern world-view, requires the belief in an afterlife which would be necessary for acceptance of the Resurrection.

By and large, it seems to me that the philosophical phase is successful, that it reveals, in fact, the prejudice of the modern age. There is one important qualification, however, which must attend my own acceptance of the argument. I think that Pannenberg goes too far in the second and third claims in arguing that modern historians should use the Resurrection as a historical account and that the modern world-view <u>requires</u> belief in an afterlife. It seems to me that what Pannenberg has actually shown is rather that belief in the Resurrection is logically consistent with (though not required by) the commitments of many modern philosophers and that belief in the Resurrection is logically consistent with the acceptance of modern historical method (though it should not be used by secular historians due to the kinds of assumptions to which they can justifiably appeal in explanations). Thus, I do not see that the considerations which Pannenberg raises could compel someone to accept the Resurrection. They do, however, remove a number of roadblocks.

As a consequence of this critical analysis, I think that the following points can be made with a fair degree of security: (1) It is no longer possible for anyone simply to say, arbiter dictum, that the Resurrection is a myth. If anyone approaches the issue in this way, he or she has not understood the biblical narrative, the human condition, or the nature of scientific and historical investigation well enough. Pannenberg is very helpful here. (2) The philosophical phase of the argument leaves one in a neutral position regarding the Resurrection. I am not in position to assess the strictly historical material. I suspect, however, that such an assessment will again leave one in a position of uncertainty. At this point, presuppositions become extremely important. If one believes on other grounds that God exists, then the evidence for the Resurrection may well be persuasive. If one does not so believe, then it does not seem to me that the evidence will be persuasive. As a point of logic, then, I suggest that the Resurrection argument does not serve well as a premise for the conclusion that God exists. Rather, belief in God serves better as a premise for the conclusion that the Resurrection occurred. (3) There is no reason why Christians should not affirm belief in the Resurrection, so long as they do not assert somehow that they know or can prove beyond reasobable doubt that it happened. This last conclusion leads directly to what appears to be, after all, the major significance of the argument in the present situation, a point of significance to which brief attention should be directed in closing the discussion.

In earlier periods in history, it could be taken for granted that professional Christian theologians would accept the historicity of the Resurrection. But that, as a study of Barth and Bultmann shows, is no longer the case. Especially among theologians who accept the historical-critical approach to the study of Scripture, it is virtually impossible to predict a stance on the Resurrection. Pannenberg's argument is important because it is worked out precisely on the assumptions of a critical approach to Scripture. If the argument is successful, even in the qualified way mentioned above, it is no slight accomplishment, for it has been by no means obvious how one could accept both a critical approach to Scripture and the Resurrection of Christ. In this way, the argument has considerable theological value in addition to its philosophical value.

For modern, critical, biblical scholarship, Pannenberg is removing certain prejudices. In the first place, he shows that the rejection of the gospel narratives of the appearances does not entail rejection of the whole idea of the Resurrection. One can still defend its historicity by focusing on the experience of Paul. In the second place, he calls into question what is sometimes dogmatically accepted by critical scholarship, namely, the presupposition that laws of nature cannot be violated. Pannenberg counters this view by showing that it depends upon a misunderstanding of the concept of natural law itself. And in the third place, he shows that there is no basis in the methodology of historical scholarship for a denial of the historical factuality of the Resurrection from the outset, and that such a procedure could cause one to overlook important data.

For the theological community especially, therefore, the argument is important. It has always been a mystery (in my opinion) how a Christian theologian could believe in the existence of God and not believe in the historicity of the Resurrection. Pannenberg has addressed that anomaly.

Philosophically, the argument is attractive though not persuasive in all respects. It does not function well as an argument for the existence of God. But it does, perhaps, enlarge the possibilities for that still-sizeable segment of the philosophical community which is generally committed to theism.

[1]This is especially remarkable in light
of the fact that Pannenberg's argument has been
available both in German and English since the
mid-sixties.

[2]Karl Barth, Church Dogmatics, ed. G. W.
Bromiley and T. E. Torrance, trans. G. T. Thomson
et al., 12 vols. (Edinburgh: T. & T. Clark,
1936-60), III/2:446-51. Barth was, of course,
ambiguous regarding the Resurrection. In early
writings he was hesitant to allow even that it
was a historical event. His final position,
as reflected in Volume Three of the Church
Dogmatics, seems to have been that it was a
historical event, but not one which could be
demonstrated to have occurred by historical
research.

[3]For Bultmann, the Resurrection represented only the "rise of faith in the risen Lord"
which was experienced by the disciples. See
his discussion in "New Testament and Mythology,"
pp. 41-42 (for publication details, see n. 10,
p. 46 above).

[4]This distinction is widely employed in
contemporary theology. It seems to have origi-
nated with the work of Martin Kähler, who makes
the distinction in his book, The So-called Historical Jesus and the Historic, Biblical Christ,
trans. with an Introduction by Carl E. Braaten
(Philadelphia: Fortress Press, 1964), pp. 62-71.

[5]"The Doctrine of Revelation," in Revelation as History, ed. Wolfhart Pannenberg, trans.
David Granskou (New York: Macmillan Company,
1968), p. 135.

[6]JGM, p. 74.   [7]Ibid., pp. 74-75.

[8]Ibid., p. 75.

[9]Ibid; the biblical reference is I Cor. 15:35-57.

[10]JGM, p. 77.   [11]Ibid., p. 76.

[12]What is Man?, p. 45. One could argue against Pannenberg that immortality is itself focused on the future in a way. It is, after all, concerned with the question what will happen after death. And in addition, it is most assuredly focused on the novel (the soul will no longer be contained in a body), though not in such a radical way, perhaps, as is the doctrine of resurrection.

[13]This claim depends on the assumption that the disciple John is not the author of the Johannine epistles.

[14]G. W. H. Lampe, "Acts," in Peake's Commentary of the Bible, ed. Matthew Black and H. H. Rowley (New York: Thomas Nelson and Sons, 1962), p. 883.

[15]JGM, pp. 92-93.

[16]Pannenberg argues that Paul was probably in Jerusalem by ca. A.D. 36, and picked up the appearance accounts from the disciples at that time (JGM, p. 90). The fact that he places his experience last on the list means that he understood their experiences to be more proximate to the Crucifixion.

[17]Ibid., pp. 96-97.

[18]Ibid; also, "Did Jesus Really Rise from the Dead?" Dialog 4 (1965):133. Here he makes contact, quite obviously, with one of the basic arguments for the Resurrection in traditional Christian apologetics. This argument does not show beyond doubt that Christ was raised, in my opinion, but the renewed fervor of the disciples remains an enigma despite the multivaried

attempts to explain it psychologically.

[19]JGM, pp. 100-101.

[20]"Did Jesus Really Rise?" p. 133.

[21]Ibid., p. 135; also, JGM, p. 98.

[22]TPS, pp. 65-66. Pannenberg makes this claim in a variety of places. See also, for instance, Faith and Reality, trans. John Maxwell (Philadelphia: Westminster Press, 1977), pp. 6-7, and in addition the entire article, "Kontingenz und Naturgesetz," in Erwägungen zu einer Theologie der Natur (Gütersloh: Gütersloher Verlagshaus Gerd Mohn, 1970), pp. 33-80.

[23]"Did Jesus Really Rise?" p. 135.

[24]Ibid.   [25]Ibid.

[26]"Kontingenz und Naturgesetz," p. 63. A nice summary discussion of this article is available in English in Frank Tupper's abovementioned work, The Theology of Wolfhart Pannenberg, pp. 217-30 (see p. 1 for publication details).

[27]"Redemptive Event and History," in BQT, 1:43. My translation differs somewhat from the English edition, and is based on the German in the original article, "Heilsgeschehen und Geschichte," in Grundfragen systematischer Theologie: Gesammelte Aufsätze (Göttingen: Vandenhoeck und Ruprecht, 1967), p. 49.

[28]"Redemptive Event and History," p. 45.

[29]Ibid., p. 48.

[30]Ibid.; also, "Analogy and Doxology," p. 231.

[31]"Redemptive Event and History," p. 49, n. 90.

[32]Herbert Burhenn, "Pannenberg's Argument for the Historicity of the Resurrection," Journal of the American Academy of Religion 40 (September 1972):375. This is by far the best treatment of Pannenberg's argument with which I am familiar. Its only limitation is that the author is concerned rather conclusively with the question of historiography.

[33]Ibid. I think that Burhenn should use "belief" rather than "knowledge" in his phrase "body of common-sense knowledge." He is obviously using "knowledge" in a very weak sense.

[34]Michael Scriven, "Truisms as the Grounds for Historical Explanations," in Theories of History, ed. Patrick Gardner (Glencoe, Ill.: Free Press, 1959), pp. 464-71.

[35]Michael Scriven, "Causes, Connections, and Conditions in History," in Philosophical Analysis and History, p. 254. The question of historical explanation is, needless to say, extremely complex. It should be noted that Burhenn has assumed that the information which a historian depends on need not be formulizable as universal laws. He does not defend this position against the Covering Law Model, and does not need to for the purpose of sustaining his criticism of Pannenberg. The objection which he makes to the latter's position could be made even more forcibly on the Hempelian assumptions.

[36]Burhenn, "Pannenberg's Argument," p. 375.

[37]This is not, of course, a denial that there are educated people who accept religious principles as part of their common-sense beliefs. That would be blatantly false. The point is, rather, that the acceptance of religious principles is not, for better or worse, widespread enough to warrant a historian's appeal to such in his or her explanations.

[38]Ibid., pp. 375-76.　　[39]Ibid., p. 372.

[40]Ibid. This, of course, is a decision of sorts. But it does not involve taking a stand on the truth or falsity of a historical claim.

[41]Non-commitment is better than an affirmative judgment strictly from the standpoint of historiography because the Resurrection is such a strange event. It would be better, Burhenn is saying, to postpone a judgment until further evidence is available, here perhaps indefinitely, than to accept something so unusual. And non-commitment is better than a negative judgment because the evidence (under our hypothesis) actually points to the truth of Christian claims that Christ was raised from the dead. It would violate the historian's objectivity to come to a negative judgment in the face of strong evidence to the contrary.

[42]This claim occurs frequently in Pannenberg's writings. See, for instance, JGM, pp. 83-88, "Did Jesus Really Rise?" p. 131, and What is Man?, pp. 41-53.

[43]JGM, pp. 81-83. He makes very strong assertions in this regard. For example,

> One must be clear about the fact that when one discusses the truth of the apocalyptic expectation of a future judgment and a resurrection of the dead, one is dealing directly with the basis of the Christian faith (pp. 82-83).

And he goes on to say that the special revelatory standing of Jesus is "incomprehensible apart from the horizon of apocalyptic expectation" (p. 83).

[44]Ibid., p. 85.　　[45]Ibid., p. 84.

[46]Pannenberg calls attention, for instance, to the importance of such belief for the mortally ill (Ibid., p. 87).

Chapter Five

GOD AND FREEDOM

No problem has been more difficult for
Christian theology than the relation between
divine power and human freedom. Many theologians have sacrificed the latter for the former;
and a few have been willing to sacrifice divine
power for human freedom. But it has often been
maintained both that God is omnipotent and that
human beings are free in the sense required to
render them morally responsible and to give them
a sense of dignity. The problem is immediately
obvious. If omnipotence is defined, as it often
is, in such a way that the power of God is thought
to range over all historical events, including
human decisions, then the latter would seem to
be functions of the divine will, or, in other
words, necessitated. And if they are necessitated,
of course, it would seem to be logically impossible to maintain that they are free in the crucial sense. Stated succinctly, then, the problem
is this: How can human beings be morally responsible and have a sense of personal dignity if
their acts are necessitated by the power of an
omnipotent God?

With characteristic candor as well as
courage, Pannenberg has addressed this issue in
many of his writings, most directly in his book,
The Idea of God and Human Freedom. Everyone
senses that Pannenberg's theology is still in
the making and that he has yet to say his final
word on this or any other major topic. Nonetheless, he has made some very provocative suggestions regarding the relation in question,
suggestions which certainly invite extensive
critical attention. In this chapter, I attempt
to state Pannenberg's argument on the relation
between God and freedom as he has developed it
to this point, and to explore what seem to me
to be the basic difficulties in such an approach.

Human Freedom

The word 'freedom', of course, has numerous meanings, and it is important to be as clear as possible from the outset about the concept of freedom which Pannenberg wants to put into play. As in other parts of his work, he attempts here to make contact with the prevailing philosophical commitments of the modern world. Reflecting generally the vast existentialist literature on freedom, Pannenberg employs the term which played an important role in the discussion of the Resurrection in the last chapter, 'Weltoffenheit', as the most apt description of the modern view of what it means to be free. In his little work in philosophical anthropology, What is Man?, he explains that 'Weltoffenheit' refers to our fundamental human orientation to the objects and events of our environment. We are originally related to this environment as "something strange" that stands over against us. We do not simply react to the things around us instinctually and thus are not simply bound to them. Rather, we react intelligently, i.e., by stepping back from the objects and events of our environment and symbolically representing them in a language. The animal's environment, in other words, becomes for the human being a world. We symbolize the environment, put our symbols together in a linguistic system, and then conceive of various projects in relation to the reality so symbolized.[1]

The trait in this human orientation to the world which primarily interests Pannenberg is our ability to transcend our own picture of things. We incorporate individuals into this picture by reference to particular contexts of meaning which are, in turn, themselves incorporated into more holistic and finally even a universal context. Not only the place of particular individuals in this world but also the world itself can be changed through the speculative inquiry of human beings. The freedom under consideration here, then, might best be called the freedom of transcendence.

Pannenberg places special importance on the turnabout in the relation between human beings and their world in the modern age. The fundamental change, he says, is this: "Man is no longer willing to fit into an order of the world or of nature, but wants to rule over the world."[2] It no longer seems sensible to us to attempt to fit into a cosmic order, for such an order itself is now perceived as a model of nature which we project for various individual and social purposes.[3] We now recognize our formative freedom in respect to the world. "The world is no longer a home for man; it is only the material for his transforming activity."[4]

Even in regard to self-understanding, we experience this same transforming freedom. Reflecting an idea similar to Sartre's concept of the 'for-itself', Pannenberg holds that the self is never at any time whole, or complete; instead, through the creative advance of reason the self is always in the process of transcending everything that it has been.[5]

There are further complexities in Pannenberg's notion of freedom, but they can be introduced later. The general contours of the freedom of transcendence are now apparent, and his question can be approached more directly. How does the power of God stack up against the self-transcendence of human beings?

The Theistic God and Freedom

Pannenberg quite clearly says that the recognition of human freedom as described above raises a serious question about the traditional conception of divine power. "In fact there is an antinomy in the attitude adopted by traditional

111

Christian theism to human freedom."[6] No solution
to the conflict could be found, he says, "as long
as the being of God was thought of as already perfect and complete in itself at every point in past
time and therefore at the beginning of all temporal processes."[7] The theistic God as often
conceived simply makes freedom in the sense of
self-transcendence impossible:

> If the eternity of God is thought of as the
> unlimited continuance of a being which has
> existed from the first, then the omnipotence
> and omniscient providence of this God must
> have established the course of everything
> that takes place in the universe in all
> its details from the very first. In this
> case there is no room for genuine freedom
> on the part of any creature.[8]

Furthermore, theology cannot ignore this
conflict, in Pannenberg's opinion, if it wishes
to present a believable conception of God. He
is well-aware of the fact that much of modern
atheism is predicated on the view that the very
idea of God is an expression of self-alienation
and a direct threat to human freedom. In the
light of this atheist critique, theology, he
says, is forced to make "a far-reaching refor-
mulation" of the idea of God.[9]

Pannenberg identifies the source of the
problem for theism with its tendency to think
of God on the analogy of "things which presently
exist" (vorhandenen Seienden).[10] Christian theology, he contends, has linked this idea of a God
fully complete in the present together with the
biblical concept of the powerful historical actions of God, and then has been unable to avoid
the unfortunate consequences of such a combination. Pannenberg does not shy away from these
consequences in any way. "Here the atheist critique is correct. A presently existent (vorhan-
denes) being who acts with omnipotence and omnis-
cience would make freedom impossible."[11]

112

How shall we understand these comments about the God who is a present reality? There is one rather direct way of understanding them, but in my opinion it represents a _faux pas_ of considerable magnitude. One might be tempted at this point to latch onto some less than circumspect remarks which Pannenberg has made regarding the nonexistence of God as a way of explicating the conflict at hand. In his programmatic work, <u>Theology and the Kingdom of God</u>, he says that in accord with New Testament eschatology the divine rule is primarily a reality of the future. Hence, "It is necessary to say that, in a restricted but important sense, God does not yet exist."[12] Also in his essay, "The God of Hope," Pannenberg makes a similar claim. He argues there that God is only God in that the divine power is demonstrated in human history. This has obviously not yet happened on a universal scale. Therefore, "Does this not mean that God does not yet exist, but is yet to be?" (<u>Gott ist noch nicht, sondern wird erst sein.</u>)[13] In the light of these claims, one is tempted to interpret the comments above about <u>Vorhandensein</u> in terms of a simplistic opposition between present and future. Under such an interpretation, Pannenberg would be saying that the present existence of an omnipotent God is incompatible with human freedom, and thus in order to preserve freedom, we should think that God does not exist, at least fully, at present but will finally exist with full power in the future.

This interpretation is obviously incorrect. In the first place, it implies either the impossible notion that God, who does not now exist, will somehow get into existence just prior to the <u>eschaton</u> or that God is now in the process of gaining power over the universe, an idea with considerable difficulties of its own. And in the second place, if God's present existence as an omnipotent being is denied in order to make room for freedom, then what is to become of the latter when God finally exists fully and completely?[14] It would seem that with the existence of God in the future, human freedom would have to be denied after all.

I believe that it is much better to understand Pannenberg's remarks about God and Vorhandensein by focusing on two characteristics which he consistently associates with the idea of the personal. A personal reality, he says, is "non-manipulable" (unverfügbar),[15] and it contains an indispensable futural dimension which is missing in nonpersonal realities.[16] Regarding the idea of non-manipulability, Pannenberg is making contact with the work of Buber. The truth in this position, in his view, is found in its efforts to understand personality by reference to "the claim of the thou."[17] If we understand a person as a power which we cannot manipulate and which exerts a claim upon our own existence, then we would distort such a reality by viewing it "in terms of the objectifying interpretation of finite entities."[18] Regarding the futural dimension of the personal, he is making contact with the work of Heidegger, Sartre, and many others, indeed the same existentialist tradition from which the notion of Weltoffenheit arises. This aspect of the concept of the personal is expressed nicely in a brief passage from Pannenberg's essay, "Speaking about God in the face of Atheist Criticism:"

> But the personality of God becomes relevant in a new way to the question of a reality which is not an existent being (vorhandenes Seiendes): a person is the opposite of an existent being. Human beings are persons by the very fact that they are not wholly and completely existent (vorhanden) for us in their reality, but are characterized by freedom, and as a result remained concealed and beyond control in the totality of their existence.[19]

114

On the basis of these comments about the futurity and non-manipulability of the personal, we can, I think, say why the modern idea of freedom is inconsistent with a view of God modelled on the analogy with Vorhandensein. And further, the inconsistency can be spelled out in two different ways, depending upon whether we begin with the assumption of the existence of God or the existence of freedom. If we begin with the former assumption (God exists without the futurity, etc., of the personal), then we must hold, argues Pannenberg, that everything in the entirety of the history of the world has already been established. The work of God, in this view, is altogether a matter of the past; there is nothing still outstanding. Freedom would be excluded in this case because God provides from the outset the world in which we have our appropriate place, and thus also the nature which we must have to be human. We could not have the freedom of self-transcendence because our nature would already be fully determined. And if we begin with the latter assumption (Freedom exists as transcendence), then we must hold, Pannenberg contends, that the God who is vorhanden can be transcended by human freedom, and thus would be something other than God.

> If freedom is the ability to go beyond that which presently exists, to set it aside or change it, then such a freedom means the ability to go beyond a God who in some way belongs to the totality of that which presently exists.[20]

A being who can be transcended by the freedom of human beings could not really be God, for such a being could not be conceived as omnipotent. "He could no longer by definition determine the freedom of man, but could be transcended by it."[21]

Through the development of this inconsistency between the power of God and human freedom, Pannenberg is pushing for a reconception of the

divine power which would take into account the
personal character of God in a much more thoroughgoing fashion than has generally been the
case in traditional theism. I shall spell out
the details of this reconception below. There
remains, however, one final ingredient which
must be included in order to get a full picture
of the problem as Pannenberg is viewing it.

Autonomy and Freedom

From our discussion so far, it sounds as
though the reconception of God is being forced
strictly from the side of the modern idea of
human freedom. That is, it sounds as though
Pannenberg has said simply that a certain view
of freedom should be accepted without critical
analysis and that the theistic conception of
God must be changed in order to accord with that
view of freedom. But this is only half of the
picture. On the other side, Pannenberg calls
attention to an inadequacy, even a breakdown,
in the modern view of freedom which makes the
idea of a personal God peculiarly suited to
the needs of our age.

Though he places great importance on the
emancipation of modern thought from "tutelage
to traditional authorities,"[22] and insists, as
we have noted already in several different places,
that the Christian religion can be relevant to
the contemporary world only insofar as theology
gives up its authoritarian strictures,[23] Pannenberg points out at the same time that the emancipated subjectivity of modern humanity has led
to problems all of its own. Autonomy by itself
is, in his view, basically a negative conception.
It focuses only on the emancipation from exter-
nal control, and is, so far as concrete content
which could give meaning to human existence is
concerned, merely an "empty formal freedom."[24]
The modern emancipated subject chooses

116

arbitrarily, whatever it wants, for its content; but since the same subjectivity is actually responsible for the content in every case, all of our choices tend to be levelled to an empty sameness in regard to the possibility of meaning. They all appear to be nothing other than just additional instances of human projections. Moreover, through such arbitrary choices, in certain social situations subjectivity has forfeited altogether the very freedom which originally was so cherished.[25]

Pannenberg says that the attempt to find a content for freedom, or to "constitute" freedom, from the standpoint of the autonomous individual is doomed to failure.[26] The breakdown in the modern conception of freedom occurs precisely at the point of the question what happens <u>after</u> emancipation. Can we establish societies and set up a convincing view of the meaning of human existence purely through the arbitrary will of the autonomous subject, or does not such a procedure reveal itself to be finally demonic and nihilistic?

The theistic tradition becomes relevant, then, to modern problems specifically in respect to the question of a content for human freedom. By this question, Pannenberg is asking how we might ground freedom, or provide a basis for it, in such a way that it cannot fall prey to the forces mentioned above. This is the other side of the issue mentioned above. It is not just that human freedom necessitates a revision in the theistic conception of God in such a way as to accentuate the personal character of the latter. It is also necessary to see the importance of the theistic view, so altered, in terms of the modern crisis in regard to human freedom. In order to come to grips with this two-sided issue, in order, in other words, to perform his hermeneutical task with integrity, Pannenberg offers his revised conception of God. The alternative to the picture of God as a fully-existent being of the present, he says, is the

picture of God as the coming reality, the reality
of the future.[27]

Divine Futurity and Human Freedom

Pannenberg takes his cue for the emphasis
on divine futurity from the eschatological interpretation of the life of Jesus which is so prominent in contemporary theology. According to this
interpretation, Jesus saw his own life in terms
of the imminent end of history. He concentrated
his ministry on the coming Kingdom of God, a
reality which he believed was already embodied
in his very existence in some way but which would
come with power in the near future. Pannenberg
extrapolates this basic structure of proleptic
anticipation of the coming Kingdom from the
experience of Jesus and applies it to universal
history itself. Christians see in Jesus in a
provisional and preliminary fashion the reality
of the coming Kingdom. The power of God in
respect to history has not yet been established
with finality, but with the Christ-event as
their basic model, Christians argue that all of
history will finally show itself to be determined
by the same reality that was apparent in Christ
himself.

Pannenberg holds that the idea of divine
omnipotence is indispensable to the Christian
faith. Indeed, as was mentioned earlier, his
most frequently-used expression for God is
'the Reality that determines everything' (die
alles-bestimmende Wirklichkeit). But the universal determinative power of God obviously elimi-
nates human freedom when such power is conceived
as a reality of the present. The eschatological
orientation of the Christian interpretation of
history, however, affords Pannenberg a novel
way in which to express the omnipotence of God,
a way which, he believes, will not only accomodate human freedom but also ground it. The
universal power of God, he suggests, should be

conceived specifically as 'the Power of the Future' (die Macht der Zukunft).

Numerous ideas are clustered around this phrase in Pannenberg's work. For our purposes, I shall focus on two of the most prominent of these: (1) the conceptual relation between the contingency of events and personal power, and (2) the notion of creation as eschaton.

In Theology and the Kingdom of God, Pannenberg provides the following summary statement of the relation between divine power and contingency:

> All experience of the future is, at least indirectly, related to God himself. In this case every event in which the future becomes finitely present must be understood as a contingent act of God. . . .Our existential awareness of the future provides evidence that our life is related to an abundant future which transcends all finite happenings. This power of the future manifests itself as a single power confronting all creatures alike. Thus this power may be properly conceived as the power unifying the world.[28]

In explication of these claims, Pannenberg points out that we are confronted by the future as an essentially-ambiguous reality. It is for us an "uncertain power" which either threatens our existence or promises a fulfillment for that existence. Our experience of the ambiguity of the future is due in part, of course, to the finite character of our knowledge of the present and past. We still do not know enough to allow for accurate predictions in most areas. But the ambiguity of the future cannot be accounted for simply by appeal to the limited state of our knowledge. "Rather, this experience of the future's ambiguity points to an essential indeterminateness or vagueness in the events of

119

nature."[29]

Here as elsewhere, Pannenberg explicitly
rejects deterministic models of reality in favor
of models which highlight the contingency of
events. In Theology and the Philosophy of Science,
he defines a contingent series as a series whose
unity can be established only by looking back
from the end.[30] This definition implies that it
is impossible in principle to establish the unity
of such a series from the outset, which in turn
can only be true if the events are not necessitated by preceding states of affairs. Thus
the ambiguity of the future depends not only on
the finite character of our present knowledge
but also on the indeterminacy built into historical development itself.

Now, Pannenberg wants to relate the idea
of God as the Power of the Future directly to
this experience of ambiguity and the contingent
nature of reality which underlies it. And the
connection is made precisely by way of the concept of personal reality. "The contingency of
events is a crucial presupposition for understanding the future as personal, and to speak
of God is to speak of a personal power."[31]
Though he does not say as much, I believe that
Pannenberg is presupposing here the idea that
a deterministic reality would not indicate the
activity of a personal source but would reflect
instead only its own abstract structures, i.e.,
the descriptive laws of science in accord with
which it invariably operates. Such a universe
would be wholly predictable and wholly unin-
teresting. And if one were able to incorporate
God into such a world, the deity would of necessity have to be conceived as a peripheral entity,
as in deism, a being who began the process but
has no interaction with it.

And on the other side, if the course of
reality were understood only as erratic and un-
connected events, it would again be impossible

to see any personal power behind them. But between the deterministic and the erratic and un-
connected universes, there is the universe of
our actual experience, a universe characterized
by the contingency of events as Pannenberg has
described it. This kind of universe, affording
room as it does both for regularities and for
the utterly unpredictable and unique, goes hand
in glove, he argues, with the concept of a personal God. The awareness of the personal in a
contingent series, he contends correctly, arises
within the context of the series and is finally
certified only by its end. To the extent that
from the end of a series of events we can see
the identity of a power operative in them by
way of meaningful connections in the events, we
perceive them as acts of a personal reality.[32]

Is there any basis for an anticipation
within the broadest of all series, history itself, to the effect that everything which happens is oriented to one final goal, or unity?
The question whether there is such a unity, in
Pannenberg's view, is the question about the
reality of God. The power which establishes
the unity of history, which can be done only
from the end, is the power over all history,
the unity toward which all reality is moving.

Pannenberg attempts to spell out this
connection between contingency and the personal
Power of the Future more closely in his novel
work on the idea of creation as eschaton, a
topic to which little attention has been accorded
in scholarly treatments of his work, but one
which, in my opinion, is at the heart of his reconception of divine power. In this connection,
Pannenberg speaks of the power of God over the
world as the power of creative love, and he
applies this understanding first to the preliminary appearance of the eschaton in Jesus
and then more generally to the process of historical development itself.

In accord with the message and actions of Jesus, the Power of the Future reveals itself to be fundamentally an attracting and receptive love. The preliminary manifestation of the Kingdom in Jesus, as Pannenberg sees it, is an expression of the love of God in that it offers to humanity an opportunity to prepare for and participate in the future rather than being overwhelmed by its sudden arrival as an alien force. The offer consists in the forgiveness of sins, an opportunity to participate in more meaningful relationships with others in the Christian community, and to develop an attitude of hope for the future, a future which includes even the promise of Resurrection, the ultimate sign of the divine love for human beings in that it shows the infinite, abiding worth of everyone. In this way, God's action in the life of Jesus opens the door for new possibilities of existence for those who respond to the offer.[33] Further, since the love of God creates these new possibilities, it is also true to say that the new existence which is the actualization of the possibilities is itself granted by the love of God.

Pannenberg explains the involvement of love in the creation not only in regard to the possibilities of existence for human beings but also, and more generally, in regard to the possibilities of existence even in the nonhuman world, though his work in this respect is not fully developed. Since each contingent event introduces new existence into the world in the new possibilities which it provides, all events, he argues, can be understood as creative acts of God's love.[34]

Now we are in position to make connection with the basic question of this chapter. How does the power of God relate to the freedom of human beings? And the answer is that the power of God consists in the divine introduction into the world of new possibilities for existence which in turn provide a basis for human freedom

in the sense of self-transcendence. And since
the Kingdom of God is futural, no present form
of knowledge or political rule can be absolutized, or identified, in effect, with the Kingdom, and thereby remove the groundwork of freedom. Pannenberg claims, then, that God as the
Power of the Future constitutes, or gives content to, human freedom in such a way that the
latter cannot fall prey to demonic forms of
bondage. He even contends that it is the predestination of God (from the end) which leads
directly to human freedom. God predestines us
to be free and open to the future through the
constant introduction of novelty into the universe, and especially of course, through the
introduction of the loving existence exemplified
by Jesus.[35]

Human beings are free, therefore, in that
God gives us a future. God may thus be conceived as the "origin of freedom" (Ursprung der
Freiheit).[36] Or as Pannenberg expresses it more
mystically, we can think of an act of God as an
act of "pure freedom" which constitutes our freedom, and the salvation which is offered to humanity as the "gift" of releasement from the
present and past.[37]

Problems in Pannenberg's Account

I do not pretend to have given an exhaus-
tive account of Pannenberg's treatment of the
issue of God and freedom, but I think that the
salient points of his treatment are before us,
and that we have enough now to allow for critical interaction. In addition, I should point
out before criticizing the position that I think
that what Pannenberg is attempting to do here is
undeniably important and interesting, and that
his work at least points in a direction which
ought to be explored more fully.

Though his synthesis of New Testament

123

eschatology and existentialist freedom is very
inviting, however, there are several questions
which should be raised in regard to his project.
I shall seek first to analyze the notion of the
determining power of the future, and then turn
attention to the issue of the relation between
Weltoffenheit and free will. And finally, I
shall discuss briefly the relation between Pannenberg's work on the issue of freedom and the
concerns of process theology generally.

The Determining Power of the Future

The claim which is fundamental to Pannenberg's novel reconception of the creation is
that it is possible for the future in some way
to determine the present and past. I shall refer
to this claim as the 'future-principle'. Before
anything else, this basic principle itself should
be called into question. What could it mean to
say that the future determines the present?

Pannenberg offers one kind of model for
understanding the future-principle which is
related specifically to the experience of human
beings. It is possible for the future to determine the present for us, he points out, due to
the fact that we are oriented to the future and
thus experience the present "in the light of a
future."[38] Since the future is an important consideration in our present experience, he argues,
"The future is thus real (wirklich), although it
is not yet present-at-hand (vorhanden)."[39]

Here Pannenberg picks up the Heideggerian
theme of the temporal character of human existence. According to this theme, the wholeness
of human life is given only by death. However,
one does not have to await death in order to
have a sense of wholeness. Rather, we can have
this sense through the very anticipation of
death as an ultimate future which cannot be

124

circumvented. The 'authentic' human existence,
says Heidegger, is one which is lived in resolute
anticipation of death, its final event.[40]

Pannenberg, of course, disagrees with
Heidegger over the ultimate destiny of humanity.
Nonetheless, he believes that the general
Heideggerian concept of the temporality of human
existence affords a way in which to understand
the determining power of the future. In Heidegger's portrait of the being of the human being,
says Pannenberg, the meaning of existence is
constituted "from the side of the future," and
this implies that the future has a kind of
"priority" (Vorrangs) for human existence.[41]

This explanation of the future-principle
shows at best how the future can be determinative
for the present for human beings only, but it
seems to me that even in this regard it is not
finally persuasive. When Pannenberg speaks of
the priority of the future for human existence,
he seems to have in mind an influence of the
future over our process of making decisions.
That is, we plan certain projects, choose one
route over another, etc., in the light of our
conception of what the future might be like.
For Christians, this means that we chart our
courses with the belief that our ultimate destiny is participation in the Kingdom of God.
That considerations pertaining to the future
play a significant role in our decision-making,
no one would deny. It is important to point out,
however, that it is not really the future itself
which influences our choices in the present;
rather, it is our ideas of what the future might
be like which influence present choices, but
these ideas, of course, are altogether present
realities. At this point, then, I suggest that
Pannenberg has conflated the idea of the future
with the future itself, and that he has explained in actuality only how one aspect of the
present, namely, one's idea of the future, is
determinative for the present.

In his essay, "Appearance as the Arrival of the Future," Pannenberg provides a different kind of explanation for the future-principle. Here he argues that if the perennial philosophical issue of the relation between appearance and essence is conceived in a temporal fashion, then appearance will be related to essence as anticipation to fulfillment. The appearance is not different from what something essentially is, for what appears is what is to come. But again, appearance is not identical to essence, for what is to come transcends appearance in the sense that the latter is only the provisional form of the former.[42]

Pannenberg admits that this position is motivated largely by the theological example of Jesus and the Kingdom. Nonetheless, he tenders it as a possibility for understanding reality in general. On behalf of his suggestion, it should be noted that this kind of relation is in fact assumed in our acquisition of scientific knowledge. A hypothesis is always a provisional statement, subject to falsification. It involves an anticipatory projection as to the truth, or essence, of the matter under consideration. On the one hand, the particular hypothesis cannot be identified with the final truth. But on the other hand, it cannot be considered irrelevant to the final truth.

In effect, Pannenberg has rendered in this case what is often construed as a vertical, ontological relation as a horizontal, historical relation. Instead of an appearance which relates to the eternal reality above it, he speaks of an appearance which relates to the temporal reality beyond it. Instead of an ontological relation, he really provides an epistemological relation. The appearance of a thing is what we know about it at present. Its essence is what we shall know about it in the future. In regard to the relation of appearance to essence, then, the priority of the future means that the essential

126

truth of things will first be known in the future, although it is anticipated through present appearances. Accordingly, the future-principle means that the future will be decisive, or definitive, for the significance of the present and past.

The best examples for this way of understanding the principle come, I believe, from the experience of viewing a play or reading a novel. The full significance of certain scenes in a play, for instance, often does not become apparent until the final act. And similarly, it is often impossible to fit together the various episodes in the early part of a novel until later in the work when a pattern begins to emerge. By analogy, Pannenberg is saying that the ultimate meaning of present and past historical events will not be known until the end of history.

This explanation of the future-principle makes it apply to everything, not just to humanity. Again it should be noted, however, that the capacity of the future to 'determine' the present in this sense of the principle has nothing to do with the exertion of an actual influence over the present. The end of a play does not somehow exert an influence over early scenes (except perhaps in the author's mind as he or she is writing the play). Rather, the end shows what the early scenes mean in connection with the whole. And by analogy, the end of history will not somehow influence events in our present. Rather, it will show the meaning of the present.

In this connection, I suggest that there is an ambiguity in the word 'determine' (and in the same way in the German 'bestimmen') which plagues Pannenberg's work on God as the Power of the Future. 'Determine' can mean 'to destine', or 'to induce', in the sense of an agent's exerting an influence over the course of events. Or it can mean 'to decide', or 'to define', in

127

the sense of someone's discovering the significance of something or in the sense of a principles's providing an important clue for the
understanding of something. Now, the future-
principle itself would seem to require the former meaning. That is, the principle claims that
the future actually exerts an influence over the
present. But in the bulk of Pannenberg's work,
including his treatment of the creation as
eschaton, for instance, he rather obviously
intends for the word to have the latter meaning.
The future determines the present in this sense
only in that it shows the essence of the present.
The following statement from Jesus--God and Man
is representative of this second interpretation
of the future-principle:

> The creation of all things, even including
> things that belong to the past, takes place
> out of the ultimate future, from the eschaton,
> insofar as only from the perspective of the
> end are all things what they truly are.[43]

And the meaning is even clearer in this statement regarding the function of Jesus in the
eschatological creation:

> Every creature receives through him as the
> eschatological judge its ultimate illumina-
> tion, its ultimate place, its ultimate defin-
> ition in the context of the whole creation.
> The essence of all events and figures is to
> be ultimately defined in the light of him
> because their essence is decided on the basis
> of their orientation to him. To that extent,
> creation of all things is mediated through
> Jesus.[44]

Pannenberg's attempt to explain the future-
principle by appealing to a temporalized version
of the appearance/reality issue, then, seems to
involve basically the notion that the future will
reveal the essence of things, or in the more
theological phraseology, the Kingdom of God as

the ultimate future of the universe determines
the significance of present events. But this
way of looking at the principle does not really
take up the notion of an actual influence of the
future over the present. Though Pannenberg develops, as we recounted above, the relations
among creative love, the contingency of events,
and personal freedom, he has not yet been able
to produce an explanation for the future-
principle itself which would facilitate our
understanding of a kind of backward-working
causality. He occasionally speaks of this
conception of causality in an almost mystical
fashion: "The future lets go of itself to bring
into being our present."[45] And again, "God in
his powerful future separates something from
himself and affirms it as a separate entity,
thus at the same time, relating it forward to
himself."[46] These statements, however, do not
serve to bring the idea to explicit expression.
And in the absence of a model by which to exp-
licate the determining power of the future in
the sense of an actual influence over the present, I submit that the concept of God as the
Power of the Future remains fundamentally unclarified.

It might be argued on Pannenberg's behalf
that he is presupposing a Hegelian-style doctrine
of universal internal relations, according to
which all of an entity's relations are essential
to it and thereby affect it in some way, and
that my analysis overlooks this important presupposition. If complete internal relatedness
were accepted, the argument might continue, then
it would be easy to see how the future determines the past. Since on this view whatever
relations anything has to anything else in its
future are constitutive for it, the future quite
obviously determines the past in the sense that
without the events in its future a thing would
be essentially different from that which it turns
out to be with such events.

I have several remarks to make concerning this particular route of defense for Pannenberg's future-principle. First, although he occasionally defers to Hegel, there is no indication in any of his writings to this point that he wants to incorporate such a doctrine of internal relations into his own work. As we have seen, in Theology and the Philosophy of Science, he devotes considerable attention to the development of a contextual theory of meaning, but a theory of meaning is quite different from a theory of being. Second, in a doctrine of complete internal relations, the future is no more important for the determination of an entity than the past, since every relation is constitutive for it. But Pannenberg's entire program implies that unless the future can be shown to be determinative for the present in a distinctive way, the existence of the God of traditional theism would preclude human freedom. And third, if the doctrine of internal relatedness were the basis for Pannenberg's views, a very serious problem regarding his way of thinking about God would result. For according to the doctrine itself, everything must be internally related to everything else. The only reality which could be independent of such relations would be Hegel's Geist, which is nothing other than the whole itself. As is obvious from the Phenomenology, there can be no independently-existing God in such a system, a being who would somehow be self-existent and unaffected by the other entities and events within the system. Hence, if Pannenberg is flirting with Hegel's doctrine, there would seem to be only two alternatives as to the way in which God could be conceived. Either God could be subordinated to the whole as an entity within it, and thus be internally related to everything else, or God could be identified with the whole, and thus be independent of everything within it. Neither view seems to have very much similarity to the biblical God of Pannenberg's works.

I suggest, therefore, that even an appeal to Hegelian metaphysical presuppositions is

ineffective in clarifying the future-principle.
It might be that the future determines the present and past in some way other than simply
showing the significance of the latter, but how
this could be remains to be seen.

Weltoffenheit and Free Will

Though it is surprising in the light of the
comments on indeterminacy noted above, Pannenberg
has very little to say about the traditional concept of free will, the capacity to choose what
one wants or to choose otherwise in a given
situation. Unless I have misunderstood his work
at this point (or unless he has changed his position recently), he does not feel that free will
plays a significant role in the generally-
existentialistic concept of freedom to which
he appeals. That is a debatable assumption.
However, whether or not free will is important
to the existentialists and thus to Pannenberg's
'modern view' of freedom, it is an abiding concern for many in the philosophical community,
and has, of course, been right at the heart of
the historical theological debate (in Augustine,
for instance) regarding God and freedom. It is
somewhat peculiar, and perhaps even indicative
of a deeper problem, that the issue of free will
is ignored.[47]

At first glance, Pannenberg's work on freedom would appear to incorporate the concept of
free will very easily. The statements which he
makes about Weltoffenheit, for instance, would
ordinarily be taken to mean that we do in fact
have free will. He says, we recall, that we
are not bound to our environment, and that the
human self is never a fixed entity but is always
transcending what it previously was. It is difficult to see how such is possible without free
will. But elsewhere, Pannenberg appears to deny
free will altogether.

The strongest comments against free will can be found in Jesus--God and Man. Here he says that it is a misconception of Jesus to think that he had "freedom of the will" to accept or oppose his divine mission. Jesus was, rather, consumed by the mission. Furthermore, he suggests that what is true for Jesus in respect to free will is likewise the case for all humanity. There is no freedom of "indifference," he says, apparently referring to the concept of free will defined above. And the "indeterminist theory of the will" is in his view a "false, one-sided representation of the reality of human freedom."[48]

Pannenberg concedes that there is an element of truth in the view that the will is free. But the element of truth turns out to be the implicit idea that human beings can transcend the present (but how, without free will?). That there is some truth in it, however, does not detract from the fact that indeterminism misrepresents the character of human choice. "In the moment of decision the will never really stands indifferently above the possibilities of choice."[49]

The issue here may be purely semantic, but I suspect that it is real. Pannenberg's portraits of the will of Christ and of human decision in general seem to indicate a rather pronounced opposition to the idea of free will. But it seems to me that without free will, both the notions of Weltoffenheit and the future, determinative power of God lose their attractiveness. If we have no free will, it really does not matter whether the determinative power in respect to our choices comes from the past, present, or the future. In any case, the choice is, after all, necessitated by a power outside ourselves, and we cannot be, as numerous philosophers have pointed out, either blameworthy or praiseworthy for such a decision. And if we have no free will, we are really bound to the past and have no freedom in the sense of a transcending openness to the future.

Perhaps the concept of free will could be incorporated into Pannenberg's approach, but it seems to me that such an addition to the position would lead to some radical revisions which would alter the basic structure of his answer. As innocent and anomalous as the omission of free will apears to be at first, I believe that it leads directly to a much more fundamental problem.

Die alles-bestimmende Wirklichkeit

and the Process God

If human beings have free will, then God may well be the Power of the Future, but God cannot be the Reality that determines everything, where 'determines' means 'exerts an actual influence over'. For on the assumption that our wills are free, we ourselves determine which way we shall decide in a given instance, and nothing, including God, determines it for us. This, in turn, implies a limitation on the divine power, either in the form of a self-limitation on the part of God, as in the theological tradition, or in the form of an inherent limitation, as in contemporary process theology.

It seems to me that the crucial ideas in Pannenberg's work on the issue of God and freedom are more at home specifically in the setting of process theology than anywhere else.[50] Here it is easily possible to speak of freedom, and indeed even of free will, because every actual occasion already has freedom built into its selective appropriation of the past. It is easy to speak of the contingency of events because the future has literally not been determined by anyone or anything. It is easy to speak of the creative character of divine love because God is precisely the source of novelty in the universe. And further, it is even easy to think of God as personal and thereby in certain respects not fully complete because in God's responsive, or as it is sometimes called, 'consequential' character, the divine reality is always in the process of actualizing values through interaction with creatures throughout the universe. But--it is impossible to think of God as omnipotent in anything like the traditional sense, because such would leave no room for the freedom of creatures or for meaningful interaction between God and creatures.

The basic problem, then, from this standpoint, is that Pannenberg's work on the futurity of God seems to require that God be thought of as limited in power and changing in certain respects. Otherwise it is difficult to see how his comments on the personal character of God really help to solve the problem at issue. Unfortunately, however, Pannenberg seems unwilling to allow for such limitations in the power of God and such developments within the very nature of God.

This point may be elucidated by reference to several remarks which he has made regarding the God or process theology. In Theology and the Kingdom of God, Pannenberg applauds both Whitehead and Hartshorne for "incorporating time into the idea of God."[51] But immediately afterward, he says, "We cannot agree when Whitehead suggests that the futurity of God's Kingdom implies a development in God."[52] He goes on to explain that from our finite, present viewpoint, it is not yet decided what the future will be, and that furthermore the movement of time actually "contributes to deciding" what the truth is going to be, even concerning God. "But--and here is the difference from Whitehead--what turns out to be true in the future will then be evident as having been true all along."[53]

134

One can only conclude from these comments that it is merely from our standpoint that there is development in God, but it is not really the case for God. This impression is shored up by Pannenberg's statement in another article to the effect that "the reality of God is still in process for every finite point of view. This does not mean that it is in the same way a process in its own terms."[54] Now it seems difficult to me to distinguish these remarks from the traditional doctrine of the impassibility of God, the belief that God is, in the final analysis, unaffected by the activities of creatures despite appearances to the contrary. At this point, Pannenberg appears to want things both ways. He wants to take the personal character of God seriously. But this implies that the reality of God must be construed as in some respects still in the process of development in itself, not just from our standpoint. He cannot, however, finally accept this idea for it betrays the infinite, transcending power of God.

The clarion call of process theology is its claim that if we seek to take the personal character of God seriously, then the God-creature relation must be viewed as internal in respect to God.[55] What we do must have some bearing, or influence, on God; it must in some way elicit a response from God. And the response indicates not just a change in the way God is to us, but in the very being of the divine reality itself. The values actualized in God are, in such a view, in part dependent upon the values actualized in creatures. They are, to be sure, originally inspired by God since the lures, or possibilities provided by the latter form a part of the basis for our motivation to act. But creatures, not God, actualize the values freely. They are not determined, as actualities, by God.

Pannenberg refuses to allow for such a move. In a discussion with the American process

135

thinker, Lewis Ford, he pointedly rejected the process interpretation in this regard.

I think there is a distinct difference between the way you and I use the phrase, "the power of the future." For you appropriate that phrase to mean that God creates the possibilities for our own self-actualization. This appropriation remains within the framework of Whitehead's metaphysics. But the implications of Jesus' message of the priority of the future of the kingdom do not have reference only to possibilities. If we endeavor to reformulate the traditional Christian idea of God in terms of the constitutive importance of eschatology, then the power of the future should not only create possibilities, but actualities as well.[56]

I submit that Pannenberg's refusal to align himself with process theology at this crucial juncture arises from a desire to preserve the idea of the omnipotence of God, even in the light of our modern preoccupation with human freedom. His phrase, 'the Reality that determines everything', is perhaps to be taken more literally than one would first expect. As it has been for many theological giants through the centuries, omnipotence is indeed of consummate importance in his concept of God. Thus, "The deity of God is his rule."[57] And again, "The assertion of a divine reality is an assertion of its power over the world and over men."[58] The possibility of a development within the nature of God has to be ruled out because it would be inconsistent with the divine omnipotence. It would imply that God is also responsive, not just creative.

In conclusion, therefore, I suggest that Pannenberg's work on the relation between divine power and human freedom, as attractive and

136

courageous as it is, runs aground in two ways. In the first place, the concept of God as the Power of the Future remains unclarified because of the absence of an acceptable explanation of the future-principle. And in the second place, the concept of freedom as Weltoffenheit does not incorporate the notion of free will in Pannenberg's approach. His God as the Power of the Future determines the present through acts of creative love. God provides a future for us and frees us for that future. But it is all the work of God. What we do causes no real changes in God, and elicits no real response from God. Whether the determinative power of God is placed, then, in the future, as in this view, or in the past and present, as in more traditional views, changes little, for human beings are not free in the crucial sense.

This is not to say that the process view of God is without flaws. There are serious problems in respect to the limitations imposed therein upon the divine actuality. And I think that Pannenberg senses the extreme difference between certain aspects of the process view and the biblical view of God Almighty. It is only to say that the sorts of moves which Pannenberg makes regarding the relation of God and freedom are more at home in the process camp. But because he persists with the model of the Reality that determines everything, his solution to the problem of God and freedom misses the issue which has been of primary importance in the process move and for the philosophical community generally, namely, Is there room for free will in a theistic universe?

NOTES

1. *What is Man?*, pp. 1-13.

2. Ibid., p. 1.   3. Ibid., p. 2.

4. Ibid.

5. "Speaking about God," p. 112; also, "Person und Subjekt," Neue Zeitschrift für systematische Theologie und Religionsphilosophie 18 (1976):144.

6. "Speaking about God," p. 107.

7. Ibid., p. 108.   8. Ibid.   9. Ibid., p. 107.

10. Ibid., p. 108. Here I deviate from the English text somewhat in order to pick up the idea of being present which seems to me to be important in the notion of Vorhandenheit. For the German reference, see "Reden von Gott angesichts atheistischer Kritik," in Gottesgedanke und menschliche Freiheit (Göttingen: Vandenhoeck und Ruprecht, 1972), p. 38.

11. "Speaking about God," p. 109. Again, I deviate slightly from the English text. See p. 40 in "Reden von Gott."

12. TKG, p. 56.

13. "The God of Hope," in BQT, 2:242. Variations from the English text are based, once more, on my interpretation of the original. For the German reference, see "Der Gott der Hoffnung," in Grundfragen systematischer Theologie, p. 393.

14. This question was raised by Professor Charles Hartshorne in response to my first attempts to explain Pannenberg's project. It shows very well the inadequacies of the interpretation under consideration. I think that

138

Pannenberg's view of God, even as the Power of the Future, is much more orthodox than one would be led to believe by the comments just cited.

[15]"The Question of God," in BQT, 2:229-30.

[16]"Person und Subjekt," p. 144.

[17]"The Question of God," p. 230, n. 99.

[18]Ibid., p. 230.

[19]"Speaking about God," p. 112.

[20]Ibid., pp. 108-9. My translation depends on the German in "Reden von Gott," pp. 39-40.

[21]"Speaking about God," p. 109.

[22]"Christian Theology and Philosophical Criticism," in BQT, 3:140.

[23]Ibid., p. 142.

[24]Ibid., p. 140; also, "Person und Subjekt," p. 136. See also his criticism of the Stoic concept of a natural, primordial freedom which has been a dominant consideration in modern political philosophy, in Human Nature, pp. 18-27.

[25]"Christian Theology," p. 141. He calls attention, for instance, to the way in which subjects often lose themselves in a world of objectivity in scientific investigation, a frequent existentialist theme. Also, Pannenberg's general critique of Marxism and other forms of social utopia expresses the same concern in a political setting. By the unbounded projection of subjectivity, freedom is easily lost.

[26]Ibid., pp. 140-41.

[27]It is important to note the dual character of the problem which Pannenberg is attempting to solve. Otherwise, one side of the hermeneutical task as he sees it will be ignored. That task is both to appropriate the tradition critically and to address the present situation of modernity critically, as we have seen.

[28]TKG, p. 61.

[29]Ibid., pp. 56-57, quote, p. 57.

[30]TPS, p. 63.   [31]TKG, p. 57.

[32]Ibid., p. 58. Pannenberg's point here seems well-taken. We often do in fact posit the involvement of a person, for instance, in everyday occurrences when we notice patterns which correspond to the sorts of things which we think an agent would do.

[33]Ibid., p. 65.   [34]Ibid., p. 66.

[35]JGM, pp. 378-97; also, Human Nature, pp. 88-94, and Faith and Reality, p. 59.

[36]"Speaking about God," p. 110.

[37]Ibid., pp. 113-14.

[38]Ibid., p. 110.

[39]Ibid. Here again, I attempt to preserve the connection between existence and presence in the German. See "Reden von Gott," p. 42.

[40]Martin Heidegger, Being and Time, trans. John Macquarrie and Edward Robinson (New York: Harper and Row, 1962), pp. 352-58.

[41]"On Historical and Theological Hermeneutic," in BQT, 1:162-74. For the German, see "Über historische und theologische Hermeneutik," in Grundfragen systematischer Theologie, p. 145.

[42]TKG, pp. 127-43.   [43]JGM, p. 230.

[44]Ibid., p. 391   [45]TKG, p. 59.

[46]Ibid., p. 70.

[47]I find this especially puzzling in the light of the fact that Pannenberg's doctoral dissertation, Die Prädestinationslehre des Duns Scotus (Göttingen: Vandenhoeck und Ruprecht, 1954), explores specifically the inconsistencies in the various Scotistic approaches to the question of predestination and condemnation.

[48]JGM, p. 352.   [49]Ibid.

[50]Lewis Ford makes the same suggestion in his article, "A Whiteheadian Basis for Pannenberg's Theology," Encounter 38 (1977):307-17.

[51]TKG, p. 62.   [52]Ibid.   [53]Ibid., p. 63.

[54]"A Theological Conversation with Wolfhart Pannenberg," Dialog 11 (1972):294.

[55]This is presupposed by the concept of the responsive love of God as outlined, for instance, in the little summary work by John Cobb, Jr., and David Ray Griffin, Process Theology (Philadelphia: Westminster Press, 1976), pp. 43-48.

[56]Wolfhart Pannenberg and Lewis Ford, "A Dialogue about Process Philosophy," Encounter 38 (1977):319.

[57]TKG, p. 55.

[58]The Apostles' Creed, trans. Margaret Kohl (London: SCM Press, 1972), p. 25.

141

CONCLUSION

The Gospel of John closes with a statement about Jesus which could be paraphrased and applied to Pannenberg. "But there are also many other things which he has written. . . ." Indeed, he has written on so many different topics that there would hardly be an end to a work which attempted to comprehend all of them. If my choice for focal issues in the present work has been meritorious, perhaps we have at least laid bare the general texture of his work, and made clear both his most significant achievements in religious philosophy to date and some of the persistent problems which have attended his work. It is time now to summarize and come to a few conclusions.

On the issue of faith and reason, we recall that Pannenberg forges a synthesis between natural reason and revelation. He denies altogether a supernatural enlightenment available only to those with the faith to see it; and yet he denies also that there can be knowledge of God apart from revelation. And the key to his synthesis is the identification of divine revelation with human knowledge.

His work on the other issues discussed shows how this synthesis is carried out in practice. The approach to hermeneutics, for instance, allows both for a critical appropriation of the tradition in the light of the present and a critical evaluation of the present conceptual framework in the light of the tradition. Neither reason nor revelation is sacrificed to the other. The purported revelation of the tradition is assessed in a radically-critical fashion; but then the presumptuous claims of modernity are also assessed just as critically. And the reason which Pannenberg brings to bear on both tradition and modernity is suffused with the notion of an ultimate revelation for universal history, a revelation

143

available in a provisional fashion in the experience of Christ.

Furthermore, by rejecting the chasm which opens when a rigid distinction is made between revelation and reason, Pannenberg is able to accomodate the contemporary awareness of the tentative character of all human knowledge. On a strictly revelational basis, theological claims have often been held in an absolutistic and dogmatic fashion. Since revelation comes specifically through human reason, in his view, there is no justification for supposing that revelational claims have to differ in terms of certainty from other kinds of claims about the world. I think that Pannenberg could go even further here by exploring in greater detail the kinship between philosophical and theological claims rather than focusing so much on the relation between scientific and theological claims. Had he explored the former relation further, I believe that he could have avoided the temptation to think of theology as a science. Pannenberg breaks up the marriage between faith and intellectual certainty, but fails to see that faith goes finally with considerable uncertainty, as Tillich and others have shown, rather than with the moderate and more tolerable lack of certainty which arises from the falsifiability of scientific statements.

In his treatment of the Resurrection, the rapprochement between reason and revelation is demonstrated most powerfully. The purported event is not made sacrosanct and available only to those who have eyes to see; rather, it is approached with the same critical, historical analysis which would be applied to any other event. And whereas philosophers, theologians, historians, and scientists have often acted as though a serious consideration of the Resurrection were beneath their intellectual dignity, Pannenberg shows how belief in it is altogether consistent with many of the prevailing beliefs

144

of modernity and the contemporary understanding
of the philosophy of science. I do not see that
he shows anywhere that belief in the Resurrection
is required if one wishes to be intellectually
honest and rigorous. But the compatibility is
quite interesting by itself. If there is such
compatibility, one can believe in the Resurrection without sacrificing his or her intellect,
and believe in the human intellect without
sacrificing revelation.

In his discussion of the question of God,
Pannenberg attempts again, as we have seen, to
synthesize widely-disparate ideas. Here he seeks
to bring together the freedom and autonomy of
the modern individual and the power of the omnipotent deity of scriptural tradition. And he
almost succeeds. It may be that the only reason
he finally pulls back in this regard is that
it simply cannot be done. It may be, that is,
that if we are free in the crucial sense, then
God simply cannot be omnipotent in the traditional sense; and if God is omnipotent in this
way, then we cannot be free. Pannenberg opts,
after all is said and done, for the latter.
At this point, the synthesis cannot bear the
tension of such radically-opposing forces.

In summary, then, the most impressive characteristics of Pannenberg's thought are its
comprehensiveness, its intellectual honesty,
and its directness and insightfulness. He never
immunizes his claims with an appeal to faith.
His work represents systematic theology as
well as religious philosophy at its best. The
basic problem, if there is one, is a consistent
tendency to incorporate too much, to attempt
to accommodate too many diversified viewpoints.
This is especially apparent in his work on
the concept of God and on theology as a science.
The basic contribution is, I think, his work
on faith and reason, especially as it is reflected in the discussions of hermeneutics and
the Resurrection.

145

I hope that this has been an enlightening
study. I wanted to bring to light Pannenberg's
work on issues of importance to the study of the
philosophy of religion, and to offer some criticisms in areas where I think further work needs
to be done. It is always easier, of course, to
criticize the work of others than to put one's
own ideas forward systematically. Many of my
own opinions have become obvious in the course
of the work, but still I have had the luxury
of being the critic, of analyzing instead of
synthesizing.

Pannenberg work is still most definitely
in progress. I hope that my critical analysis
will serve to sharpen the debate in the theological and philosophical communities on the
questions at issue, and perhaps even be
of value to Pannenberg in his continuing
project.

A SELECTED BIBLIOGRAPHY

I. Works of Pannenberg

The Apostles' Creed: In the Light of Today's
    Questions. Translated by Margaret Kohl.
    Philadelphia: Westminster Press, 1972.
    A translation of Das Glaubensbekenntniss,
    ausgelegt und verantwortet vor der Fragen
    der Gegenwart. Hamburg: Siebenstern
    Taschenbuch Verlag, 1972.

Basic Questions in Theology: Collected Essays.
    3 vols. Vols. 1 and 2 translated by
    George H. Kehm. Philadelphia: Fortress
    Press, 1970-71. A translation of Grund-
    fragen systematischer Theologie: Gesam-
    melte Aufsätze. Göttingen: Vandenhoeck
    und Ruprecht, 1967. Vol. 3 translated
    by R. A. Wilson. London: SCM Press, 1973.
    Also published under the title, The Idea
    of God and Human Freedom. Philadelphia:
    Westminster Press, 1973. A translation
    of Gottesgedanke und menschliche Freiheit,
    Göttingen: Vandenhoeck und Ruprecht, 1972,
    plus several additional articles.

"Christologie und Theologie," Kerygma und Dogma
    21 (Juli/September 1975):159-75.

"Did Jesus Really Rise from the Dead?" Dialog
    4 (1965):128-35. A translation of "Ist
    Jesus wirklich auferstanden?" Geistliche
    Woche für Südwest-Deutschland der Evan-
    gelischen Akademie Mannheim (Februar 16-23,
    1964):22-33.

"Dogmatic Theses on the Doctrine of Revelation,"
    in Revelation as History, pp. 123-58.
    Edited by Wolfhart Pannenberg, et al.
    Translated by David Granskou. New York:
    Macmillan Company, 1968. A translation of

147

Offenbarung als Geschichte. Edited by
Wolfhart Pannenberg. Göttingen: Vandenhoeck und Ruprecht, 1961.

"Einheit der Kirche und Einheit der Menschheit,"
in Um Einheit und Heil der Menschheit.
Herausgegeben von J. Robert Nelson und
Wolfhart Pannenberg. Frankfurt am Main:
Verlag Otto Limbeck, 1973.

"Future and Unity," in Hope and the Future of Man,
pp. 60-78. Edited by Ewert H. Cousins.
Philadelphia: Fortress Press, 1972.

"Der Gott der Geschichte," Kerygma und Dogma
23 (April/Juni 1977):76-92.

Human Nature, Election, and History. Philadel-
Westminster Press, 1977.

Jesus--God and Man. Translated by Lewis L.
Wilkins and Duane A. Priebe. Philadelphia:
Westminster Press, 1968. A translation of
Grundzüge der Christologie. Gütersloh:
Gütersloher Verlagshaus Gerd Mohn, 1964.

"Kontingenz und Naturgesetz," in Erwägungen zu
einer Theologie der Natur, pp. 33-80.
Gütersloh: Gütersloher Verlagshaus Gerd
Mohn, 1969.

"Person und Subjekt," Neue Zeitschrift für
systematische Theologie und Religionsphilosophie 18 (1976):133-48.

Die Prädestinationslehre des Duns Skotus.
Göttingen: Vandenhoeck und Ruprecht, 1954.

Reality and Faith. Translated by John Maxwell.
Philadelphia: Westminster Press, 1977.
A translation of Glaube und Wirklichkeit.
Munich: Christian Kaiser Verlag, 1975.

Reformation zwischen gestern und morgen (Gütersloh: Gütersloher Verlagshaus Gerd Mohn, 1969.

"Response to the Discussion," in Theology as
     History, pp. 221-76. Edited by James M.
     Robinson and John B. Cobb, Jr. New York:
     Harper and Row, 1967.

"The Revelation of God in Jesus of Nazareth,"
     in Theology as History, pp. 101-33.
     Edited by James M. Robinson and John B.
     Cobb, Jr. New York: Harper and Row, 1967.

Spirit, Faith, and Church. Philadelphia: West-
     minster Press, 1970.

"Die Subjektivität Gottes und die Trinitäts-
     lehre," Kerygma und Dogma 23 (Januar/
     März 1977):25-40.

"A Theological Conversation with Wolfhart
     Pannenberg." Dialog 11 (1972):286-95.

"Theologische Motive im Denken Immanuel Kants."
     Theologische Literaturzeitung 89 (1964):
     897-906.

Theology and the Kingdom of God. Edited by
     Richard John Neuhaus. Philadelphia:
     Westminster Press, 1969.

Theology and the Philosophy of Science. Philadel-
     phia: Westminster Press, 1976. A trans-
     lation of Wissenschaftstheorie und Theo-
     logie. Frankfurt am Main: Suhrkamp Verlag,
     1973.

What is Man? Contemporary Anthropology in
     Theological Perspective. Translated by
     Duane A. Priebe. Philadelphia: Fortress
     Press, 1970. A translation of Was ist
     der Mensch? Die Anthropologie der Gegen-
     wart im Lichte der Theologie. Göttingen:
     Vandenhoeck und Ruprecht, 1962.

Anderson, James F. The Bond of Being. St.
     Louis: Herder Book Company, 1949.

_____. Reflections on the Analogy of Being.
     The Hague: Martinus Nijhoff, 1967.

Barth, Karl. Church Dogmatics. 12 vols. Edited
     by G. W. Bromiley and T. F. Torrance.
     Translated by G. T. Thomson et al.
     Edinburgh: T. & T. Clark, 1936-60.

Bultmann, Rudolf. "New Testament and Mythology,"
     in Kerygma and Myth. 2 vols. Vol. 1,
     pp. 1-44. Edited by Hans-Werner Bartsch.
     Translated by Reginald H. Fuller. London:
     SPCK, 1953-62.

Burhenn, Herbert. "Pannenberg's Argument for
     the Historicity of the Resurrection,"
     Journal of the American Academy of
     Religion 40 (September 1972):368-79.

Cobb, John B., and David Ray Griffin. Process
     Theology: An Introductory Exposition.
     Philadelphia: Westminster Press, 1976.

Dilthey, Wilhelm. Pattern and Meaning in
     History. Edited by H. P. Rickman.
     London: Allen and Unwin, 1961.

Ford, Lewis S. "A Whiteheadian Basis for Pan-
     nenberg's Theology," Encounter 38 (1977):
     307-17.

_____, and Wolfhart Pannenberg. "A Dialogue
     about Process Philosophy," Encounter 38
     (1977):318-24.

Gadamer, Hans-Georg. Truth and Method. Trans-
     lated and edited by Garrett Barden and John
     Cumming. New York: Seabury Press, 1975.

Gilkey, Langdon. "Review of Basic Questions
     in Theology," Perspective 14 (Spring 1973):
     34-55.

Harvey, Van Austin. The Historian and the
     Believer. New York: Macmillan Company,
     1966.

Hegel, G. W. F. Lectures on the Philosophy
     of Religion. 3 vols. Translated by
     E. B. Spiers and J. B. Sanderson. New
     York: Humanities Press, 1962.

_____. The Phenomenology of Mind. Translated by
     J. B. Baillie. London: Allen and Unwin,
     1949.

Heidegger, Martin. Being and Time. Translated
     by John Macquarrie and Edward Robinson.
     New York: Harper and Row, 1962.

Hick, John. Philosophy of Religion. Englewood
     Cliffs, N. J.: Prentice-Hall, 1963.

Jensen, Robert W. God after God: The God of
     the Past and of the Future as seen in the
     Work of Karl Barth. New York: Bobbs-
     Merrill Company, 1969.

Johnson, S. E. "Son of Man," in The Inter-
     preter's Dictionary of the Bible. 4 vols.
     Vol. 4, pp. 413-20. New York: Abingdon
     Press, 1962.

Kähler, Martin. The So-called Historical Jesus
     and the Historic, Biblical Christ. Trans-
     lated with an Introduction by Carl E.
     Braaten. Philadelphia: Fortress Press,
     1964.

Kant, Immanuel. Critique of Pure Reason. Trans-
     lated by Norman Kemp Smith. New York:
     St. Martin's Press, 1965.

_____. Religion within the Limits of Reason
Alone. Translated by Theodore M. Greene
and Hoyt H. Hudson. New York: Harper and
Brothers, 1960.

Lampe, G. W. H. "Acts," in Peake's Commentary
of the Bible, pp. 882-926. Edited by
Matthew Black and H. H. Rowley. New
York: Thomas Nelson and Sons, 1962.

Moltmann, Jürgen. Theology of Hope: On the
Ground and the Implications of a Christian Eschatology. Translated by James
W. Leitch. New York: Harper and Row,
1967.

Neuhaus, Richard John. "Profile of a Theologian," in Theology and the Kingdom of
God, by Wolfhart Pannenberg, pp. 9-50.
Edited by Richard John Neuhaus. Philadelphia: Westminster Press, 1969.

Ogden, Schubert. Christ Without Myth. New
York: Harper and Brothers, 1961.

Pasquariello, Ronald D., "Pannenberg's Philosophical Foundations," Journal of Religion
56 (October 1976):338-47.

Passmore, John A. "The Objectivity of History,"
in Philosophical Analysis and History,
pp. 75-94. Edited by William H. Dray.
New York: Harper and Row, 1966.

Peters, Ted. "Truth in History: Gadamer's
Hermeneutics and Pannenberg's Apologetic
Method," The Journal of Religion 55
(January 1975):36-56.

Schmid, Heinrich. The Doctrinal Theology of the
Evangelical Lutheran Church. 3rd ed.
Translated by Charles A. Hay and Henry
E. Jacobs. Minneapolis: Augsburg Pub-
lishing House, 1875.

Scriven, Michael. "Causes, Connections, and Conditions in History," in Philosophical Analysis and History, pp. 238-64. Edited by William H. Dray. New York: Harper and Row, 1966.

_____. "Truisms as the Grounds for Historical Explanations," in Theories of History, pp. 443-73. Edited by Patrick Gardner. Glencoe, Ill.: Free Press, 1959.

Strawson, P. F. "On Referring," in Logico-linguistic Papers, pp. 1-27. London: Methuen and Company, 1971.

Tupper, Frank. The Theology of Wolfhart Pannenberg. Philadelphia: Westminster Press, 1972.

Wittgenstein, Ludwig. Philosophical Investigations. 3rd ed. Translated by G. E. M. Anscombe. New York: Macmillan, 1968.

INDEX

Afterlife, 95-99
Analogy, 4, 36-45; of
    attribution, 37; of
    proportionality, 37;
    principle of in his-
    tory, 89-90
Analytic philosophy, 4,
    72
Appearances of Jesus,
    78, 81-84
Appearance and reality,
    126
Aristotle, 10
Atheism, 112
Autonomy, 15-16, 21,
    116-18

Barth, Karl, 4, 9-10,
    27-28, 40, 51, 75,
    103
Bultmann, Rudolf, 4,
    9-10, 25-28, 40,
    46, 51, 53-54, 75,
    103
Burhenn, Herbert, 91-
    93, 106

Context, 4, 23-45,
    significance for
    meaning, 23-28,
    significance for
    truth, 28-35
Contingent events, 119-
    121
Creation as eschaton,
    121-23, 128

Death, 85-89
Determine, meaning of,
    127-28
Dialectical theology,
    9-10, 75-76

Dilthey, Wilhelm, 12
Doxology, 39-41
Dualism, 76

Empty tomb, 83-84
Eschatology, 11, 27;
    and verification,
    41-45
Eschaton, 35-36, 42-
    45, 121-23
Existentialism, 96-99

Faith, 11; elements
    of, 13; logic of, 13
Ford, Lewis, 136, 141
Freedom, problem of,
    109; of transcen-
    dence, 110-11; and
    God, 109-37
Fusion of horizons,
    30-33
Future, 19, 32-35;
    determining power
    of, 124-31
Futurity, of the per-
    sonal, 114-16; of
    God, 118-23

Gadamer, Hans-Georg,
    30-35, 47, 56
God, concept of, 109-
    37; origin of free-
    dom, 123; Power of
    the Future, 119-23;
    the Reality that
    Determines every-
    thing, 118, 133-37;
    theology as a science
    of, 53-55; and
    natural laws, 87

Hegel, G. F. W., 12, 129

155

Heidegger, Martin, 97-
98, 114, 124-25
Hermeneutics, 4, 23-45,
47, 61, 116-18, 140,
143
Historical reason, 12-
13
Historiography, 89-95
History, influence of
and truth, 65-66;
statements about,
60-62; and the
Resurrection, 81-84;
of religions, 52

Immortality, 79-80, 104
Impassibility, 135
Internal relations,
129-30

Jesus Christ, appearance
to Paul, 78, 81-84;
and openness to the
future, 66-67; pro-
leptic manifestation
of the Kingdom in,
121-23; historical
as opposed to the
Christ of faith, 76

Kant, Immanuel, 10, 12,
20, 54
Kierkegaard, Søren, 98
Kingdom of God, 121-23
Knowledge, 14, 17

Language games, 24
Laws of science, 84-87
Luther, Martin, 10
Lutheran rationalism,
14-15

Meaning, 23-28; and
reference, 24

and intention, 24
Metaphysics, 12

Natural sciences, 55-
57, 84-88
Natural theology, 4, 10
Neuhaus, Richard John,
1

Objectivity, 55-56, 69-
70

Passmore, John, 69
Paul, 78, 81-84, 104
Person, concept of, 114
Peters, Ted, 47
Phenomenology, 52
Philosophy, statements
of, 62-71; and the
Resurrection, 84-102
Plato, 11
Pluralism, 64-65
Popper, Karl, and
Thomas Kuhn, 47
Process philosophy, 5-6,
133-37; Hartshorne,
134, 138; Whitehead,
134

Rationality, Pannen-
berg's, 2-3
Reason, concepts of,
10-12, 19
Reformation, 15
Relativism, 29-36
Resurrection, 5, 11,
75-102, 144-45;
meaning of, 77-80;
and immortality, 79-
80; and resuscita-
tion, 78-79

Sartre, Jean-Paul, 97-
98, 111, 114

Scripture, critical
    approach to, 101-102
Scriven, Michael, 92,
    106
Social sciences, 55-56

Theology, as a science,
    2, 5, 51-71
Thomas Aquinas, 10, 48
Truth, and consensus,
    29; and correspon-
    dence, 29; in rela-
    tion to context,
    28-36; historical

nature of, 29
Tupper, Frank, 1, 48

Universal history,
    32-36

Verifiability, 4, 36-
    45, 55-64

Weltoffenheit, 62, 73
    95-99, 110-11, 131-
    33
Wittgenstein, Ludwig,
    24, 28